ANALYZING THE ISSUES

CRITICAL PERSPECTIVES ON
FEMINISM

Edited by Anne C. Cunningham

Enslow Publishing

101 W. 23rd Street
Suite 240
New York, NY 10011
USA

enslow.com

Published in 2018 by Enslow Publishing, LLC
101 W. 23rd Street, Suite 240, New York, NY 10011

Library of Congress Cataloging-in-Publication Data

Names: Cunningham, Anne C, editor.
Title: Critical perspectives on feminism / edited by Anne C. Cunningham.
Description: New York : Enslow Publishing, [2018] | Series: Analyzing the issues | Audience: Grade 9 to 12. | Includes bibliographical references and index.
Identifiers: LCCN 2017001288 | ISBN 9780766084810 (library-bound)
Subjects: LCSH: Feminism--Juvenile literature. | Feminists--Juvenile literature.
Classification: LCC HQ1155 .C758 2018 | DDC 305.42--dc23
LC record available at https://lccn.loc.gov/2017001288

Printed in China

To Our Readers: We have done our best to make sure all website addresses in this book were active and appropriate when we went to press. However, the author and the publisher have no control over and assume no liability for the material available on those websites or on any websites they may link to. Any comments or suggestions can be sent by e-mail to customerservice@enslow.com.

Excerpts and articles have been reproduced with the permission of the copyright holders.

Photo Credits: Cover, Brian Ach/WireImage/Getty Images (Gloria Steinem), Thaiview/Shutterstock.com (background, pp. 4–5 background), gbreezy/Shutterstock.com (magnifying glass on spine); p. 4 Ghornstern/Shutterstock.com (header design element, chapter start background throughout book).

CONTENTS

INTRODUCTION

Feminism refers to any collective political action or social movement to establish women's political rights, economic prospects, educational opportunities, bodily autonomy, and personal freedom. Though this definition is a good starting point, contemporary feminism encompasses far more than rights and equality for women exclusively. Emerging from the so-called "third wave" of feminism, which began in the 1990s, a new paradigm called intersectional feminism posits that all forms of systemic oppression are interconnected and inseparable. Intersectional thought and activism seeks common ground across disparate struggles, and strives for fundamental unity amongst all subjects desiring social justice and full personhood in societies skewed toward classism, sexism, and white privilege.

Deploying various methods, contemporary feminist thought focuses primarily on changing unjust societal conditions, while downplaying any emphasis on self-actualization or "having it all" espoused by the preceding generation of feminists, collectively known as the "second wave." These thinkers came of age during the relatively affluent and hopeful 1960s and 1970s, and despite their many valuable contributions, particularly with respect to women's reproductive rights, second-wave feminists are now often criticized for universalizing the white, heterosexual, middle class female subject. In our first article, Aalya Ahmad identifies these concerns, but cautions against the neat categorization of feminism into distinct waves. There is much overlap between schools of feminist thought, and generational conflict should not obscure the commonalities feminists have shared throughout the ages.

Although the word "feminism" did not enter popular parlance until the utopian socialist Charles Fourier first coined the term in nineteenth-century France, there have likely been feminists ever since women first reflected on and questioned their place in society—which is to say, since ancient times, and possibly earlier. Likewise, once women began cooperating to achieve these goals, some form of feminism has existed. We have good reason to believe this. Institutionalized male dominance, also known as patriarchy, has largely excluded women from full political participation and citizenship through much of world history. True, there have been notable female political leaders, ranging from Queen Hatshepsut of Egypt to Theodora of Constantinople. While the presence of female heads of state sometimes bodes well for women, the relationship is not always direct. For example, it would be difficult to argue that Margaret Thatcher's politics were feminist, as they did not benefit the majority of Britain's women or working class. All too often, female leaders are exceptions that prove the rule of rampant sexism. In our second chapter, Peter Bloom examines Hillary

Clinton's presidential bid from this angle. Bloom recognizes the historic, inspiring potential that her campaign evoked. However, her mixed record on social issues, militarism, and economic elitism are quite troubling from a feminist perspective.

However problematic of an understanding of intersectional feminism Clinton displayed, her record as a champion of women's issues such as legal abortion rights and equal pay is unimpeach-able. Given the immense pushback mounted by Republican lawmakers against *Roe v. Wade*, which legalized abortion throughout the United States, a Clinton victory would have given all but the most radical feminists cause for relief. Instead, given Donald Trump's electoral win, feminists are growing fearful that abortion rights will continue to be rolled back. The Supreme Court recently heard a case in which a Texas-based abortion clinic, Whole Woman's Health, sued the Texas Department of State Health Services for placing onerous restrictions on abortion clinics. Texas House Bill 2 (HB 2) imposed expensive and unnec-essary operating costs on abortion clinics with the tacit aim of shutting them down. The high court ruled in favor of Whole Woman's Health, but push-back is likely to continue. The full effect that a Trump presidency will have on abortion rights—and, more broadly, women's rights—remains to be seen.

One might assume that feminism's core message of social justice would appeal to far more Americans today than it currently does. As income inequality, environmental injustice, and institutionalized racism show no signs of abating, a movement that addresses these problems, however imperfectly, should have near universal value. Puzzlingly, less than one quarter of Americans polled in 2014 identify as feminists. As 82 percent agree with the core tenets of feminism, these results suggest that feminism is perhaps misunderstood. Some blame the media for presenting a version of feminism that is too heroic or confrontational for average women to embrace. Others suggest that the term "feminist" places undue emphasis on identity, and prefer terms such as "advocating for feminism" or "doing feminism."

Regardless of semantics, if women are to keep their hard-won rights and gain new ones, a clear understanding of what feminism is, and what it can do, is essential. We hope this reader provides you with valuable insights to this end.

CHAPTER 1

WHAT ACADEMICS, EXPERTS, AND RESEARCHERS SAY

One of feminism's primary aims is to critique and dismantle systems of oppression, including, but not limited to, patriarchy. Those who advocate for feminism typically concur that solidarity is essential to the struggle for social justice. Nonetheless, feminism today is a highly fractured discourse.

This chapter will trace a few of the fault lines within contemporary feminism from the point of view of experts and academics working in the field. Before we begin, one initial caveat is in order: some feminists are skeptical of the specialized language upon which expert opinions rest. Aalya Ahmad's article "Feminism Beyond The Waves: Do We Need

A Different Metaphor Than Three Big Waves To Appreciate Feminism Today?" cites Alexandra Nuttal's claim that "[a]cademic feminism is hierarchy-based, privileged, and rests on your command of the key terms." While this view perhaps reinforces the stereotype of academic elitism, Nuttal's point is that feminism need not be overly theoretical to have value. Of course this works both ways. For example, despite intersectional feminism's origin as an academic discourse, the concept is now widely understood and operative among grassroots feminist activists.

Feminism has been subject to criticism for privileging white, middle and upper class, able-bodied, heterosexual women, while excluding those who do not fit this narrow profile. Often-times, white women have been critiqued for calling for equal power to white men, without working to change the oppression that women of color face. The first-wave feminists of the nineteenth century exemplified this approach. They sought equal civil and political rights, such as the right to hold property, vote, and run for office, but did not radically challenge the status quo. Second-wave feminists augmented this agenda with a far-reaching critique of patriarchy, stronger advocacy for reproductive rights such as abortion and contraception, and an emphasis on sexual freedom. Currently, third-wave feminists have expanded the feminist critique to include all overlapping systems of oppression, from the extraction of natural resources, to the violent policing of African-American men. Despite the convenience of the waves metaphor, some caution against its too neat rendering of disparate feminist practices.

To some, feminism is tantamount to a radical transformation of all systematized tools of societal oppression. Others, such as Deborah Spar, retain a focus on more traditional articulations of feminism, such as equal pay and career-family balance within a basic capitalist framework. It is perhaps cliché to say there are as many feminisms as there are individual women (and men, as Scott Taylor's article demonstrates), but for a movement that both thrives on unity and is especially vulnerable to divisiveness, finding common ground and ways to communicate across identities remains a prerequisite for feminist progress.

"FEMINISM BEYOND THE WAVES: DO WE NEED A DIFFERENT METAPHOR THAN THREE BIG WAVES TO APPRECIATE FEMINISM TODAY?" BY AALYA AHMAD, FROM *BRIARPATCH*, JUNE 30, 2015

Feminism isn't dead. In fact, recent news tends to present feminism as Lady Lazarus, being "reborn" in the dazzling invocations of Beyonce, the impassioned addresses of actor Emma Watson, and the executive leanings-in of Sheryl Sandberg. Beyond the advocacy of celebrity culture, Pakistani activist Malala Yousafzai and the mass abduction of the Chibok schoolgirls in Nigeria have raised the issue of girls' equal access to education. At home, outrage mounts over the Conservative government's refusal to address the systemic issue of hundreds of missing and murdered Indigenous women and girls, as well as its stubbornly sexist resistance to implementing a desperately needed national child-care program.

Despite these issues and so many more, non-elite feminist voices are often trivialized or ignored. Last year, for example, *Toronto Star* columnist Heather Mallick asked, "Where are Canada's prominent young feminists, if it has any active, prominent feminists at all?" In a response piece, I wrote: "Heather, we're everywhere. Feminists might not be jutting out of the national landscape like those gloriously phallic Lawren Harris icebergs. We're more like stars in the northern skies: if you don't see us, you might not be looking long or hard enough, or maybe there's something else getting in the way."

What was getting in the way? How on earth could Mallick possibly miss the young feminists in the Miss G

Project for Equity in Education, Hollaback, and SlutWalk? What about Idle No More, the Maple Spring, Occupy, and other mass uprisings chock full of strong activists concerned with gender and equality issues? Just how prominent and famous do you have to be to be a feminist, anyway? And exactly what sorts of feminism are you supposed to be active in to get some respect?

LOOKING BACK ON THE WAVES

How we talk about social movements matters. Mallick's obliviousness to the existence of young feminists today raises the question of the power of metaphors to frame our struggles. The idea that there have been at least three waves of feminism in the Global North has been highly influential, but can we still speak of waves of feminism now? What does it mean to think of ourselves as feminists in waves? Who does that leave out?

The First Wave – roughly spanning the 19th century to the first quarter of the 20th – focused on civil and political rights: legal personhood and the rights to inherit and hold property, vote, run for office, and access higher education. These rights were at first enjoyed only by white, middle- or upper-class women, but were gradually won – on paper, at least – by all. The Second Wave reached its zenith in the 1970s. Women organized to raise consciousness of their unequal conditions, and named and challenged patriarchy and structures of everyday oppression (the family, the workplace, electoral politics). They marched, lobbied for child care, reproductive rights, and equal pay, and set up committees, collectives, and centres devoted to safeguarding and advancing hard-won rights (rape crisis and battered women's shelters, health and legal clinics). Feminists confronted sexism in clever and creative ways, such as the "Freedom Trash Can" at the Miss America Pageant (the origin of the myth of the bra-burner). The Second Wave defined feminism as a revolutionary politics, a transformative politics, and above all, as a mass politics. By the 1980s, feminism was facing a strong backlash but was also firmly entrenched as more women entered workplaces and universities.

The Third Wave of the 1990s applied the concept of intersectionality to ongoing systemic issues of gendered oppression. Feminism was again defined as a transformative politics, challenging what Third Wavers saw as an overly narrow focus on sexism. However, the Third Wave also saw the retreat of organized feminism to certain institutional safe havens (the academy, NGOs, labour unions, and policy think tanks), resulting in feminism's professionalization and institutionalization under neoliberal capitalism. There is a sense in which "professional" feminism has been relegated to legislative and policy arenas, with feminists redefined as technocratic specialists on "women's issues" rather than revolutionaries.

NO WAVE FEMINISMS

Feminist theorist Victoria Bromley writes, "The wave metaphor offers us a sense of feminist continuity," and this sentiment is reflected in some of the responses from the five feminist activists I interviewed for this article. "I think the concept of waves was helpful for a while," Julie Lalonde of Hollaback! says. "It's certainly great for looking back on feminist organizing historically."

While feminist radio show host Alexandria Nuttal allows that "waves are a convenient way of splitting up in order to understand history," she points out that the academic feminist tendency to historicize the movement as waves reinforces the idea of people as books: "Did the book change to include another chapter or a new chapter? Did we all read the same book? Why does that matter?"

Bromley cautions, "The wave metaphor tends to emphasize mainstream feminist movement while eclipsing groups of feminists that don't fit comfortably into the imagined mainstream of [the] white, middle-class, heterosexual, able-bodied women's movement." When asked if the concept of feminist waves was relevant to her work, Indigenous activist Leanne Simpson confirms this point: "Indigenous feminisms are No Wave feminisms and are intrinsically a result of and a connection to colonialism and settler colonialism, which brought to our nations white supremacy, heteropatriarchy, and capitalism. Gender[ed] colonial violence has been a primary tool and strategy on the part of the states to attack and remove our bodies from our homelands."

Rather than connecting her work to waves of feminism, Simpson links it to "400 years of Indigenous resistance to colonialism ... taking on issues of dispossession and displacement, erasure, capitalism, and gender violence. I am always connected [to] and building upon the work of my Ancestors and those that have gone before – revolutionary thinkers like Lee Maracle and Ellen Gabriel, but also youth who are doing really radical work on the ground." Lalonde likewise speaks of "feminist foremothers." Creative resistance by groups like the Radical Handmaids is directly tied to things like Canada's 'Abortion Caravan,' she says.

The Ontario Coalition Against Poverty's Liisa Schofield observes, "I don't often find myself thinking about feminism and feminist history in waves. Instead I choose to look at feminist history with the hope of finding inspiration in the ways women have always resisted patriarchy and other systems of oppression. I aim to take leadership from Indigenous feminists, feminists of colour, and revolutionary socialist and anarchist women who are often written out of mainstream histories of feminism."

Simpson laments the lack of visibility and resources for Indigenous feminist organizations, which can be linked to this erasure: "I notice they are doing incredible work with very little support. I notice that it is difficult to get their voices and perspectives into the mainstream media. I notice that other organizations do a lot of speaking on behalf of – rather than amplifying or including the voices of – women most impacted by the issues they are speaking about."

FEMINIST HIERARCHIES

Unfortunately, hierarchies of perfection have appeared within feminism, says Nuttal. And the power dynamics and terms of exclusion differ depending on sector, causing a lack of entry points to feminisms at all levels. "Academic feminism is hierarchy-based, privileged, and rests on your command of the key terms," she reflects, "whereas in grassroots feminism a lot depends on the networks you have, the credentials you've accumulated." In grassroots activism, there is "the idea that I should be able to recognize you as a feminist and if not, you're a nobody."

Miss G organizer Dilani Mohan points to the existence of a "call-out culture right now that just lends itself to inertia. People who would otherwise act or speak are almost pre-emptively shamed into silence." For Nuttal, such an emphasis on hierarchies of knowledge and feminist "cred" "takes our politics out at the knees." Similarly, Lalonde remarks, "I wish the adversities came from outside only, but sadly, many of them come from within as well. Internal conflict, dog-eat-dog competition, and turf wars are alive and well in social justice circles, sadly."

Such talk of competition and the cultural capital of professionalized feminist knowledge reminds us that, as Schofield says, "class matters" and real lives are at stake, not just theoretical territory. "Theory is beautiful and wonderful," Schofield tells me, "but we also need direct action and on-the-ground struggle for tangible gains ... In feminism today, we continue to see the lives of the poorest women swept to the side and not addressed. We internalize and perpetuate notions of the 'deserving and undeserving' poor – that some women are deserving of services or not, deserving of safe space or not. We need to see the inter- sections of patriarchal violence, trauma, poverty, colonialism and capitalism. Fighting for housing, shelter, or drop-in space is a feminist issue. Access to services for people regardless of immigration status is a feminist issue. Access to safe consumption sites is a feminist issue. Decriminalizing sex work is a feminist issue ... I don't know exactly where we are now, but I hope that we are coming to a place, at least in Toronto, and ideally across these territories, where intersec- tionality and decolonization are truly practised, and where we are trans inclusive and sex worker positive and that to be otherwise is plain anti-feminist."

In all cases, "the key to successful feminist orga- nizing is tenacity," says Lalonde. "Keep knocking on the door, smashing the ceiling, and pushing forward, regardless of whether people think it's a waste of time or not. The work is worth doing. It's always, always worth doing."

A FEMINIST ECOSYSTEM

Many of us have grown accustomed to thinking of social movements as great forces that crash and burst over society, leaving irrevocable change in their wake. The struggles of feminists to have their work recognized show us that this is a misleading idea that can actually undermine our ability to see what is really going on. Perhaps it's time to honourably retire the concept of feminist waves, at one time so useful and important.

Symbolically, the wave metaphor presents a false idea of unity, depersonalizes the hard work that people perform on a daily basis to bring about change, and romantically exalts certain tactics and forms of struggle – mass rallies, for example, which try to visually demonstrate that great wave, that rolling mass of people. But many mass rallies, at least in North America, now feel hollow and contrived; people dutifully and symbolically gathering in front of empty offices for finite periods, then just as dutifully returning to their homes and workplaces. Do these tactics still accurately reflect all the varied shapes of our social movements? Nuttal tells me, "I'm not into protests and marches – that makes me feel uncomfortable. There's no conversation happening there – people screaming slogans at each other. As a cultural feminist, I like providing space for growth, for conversation." It took her a long time to realize, she says, that this was activism too.

Says Mohan: "I like to think of activism today as more of a ripple than a wave. Waves are singular and impressive in their force. That does not mean that ripples cannot accomplish the same lands of things that waves can. In fact, if I have my geographic/ geologic knowledge straight, constant currents, ripples or tides, can permanently change a landscape or the direction of a river. We each act in different ways but we come up against that same shore all the same, and we each break down just a bit of it. The end result may very well be identical to a wave, but in a way that allows us all to devote our attention to making the changes that we feel are necessary to our lived experiences and understanding of the world."

Feminists may no longer want to imagine movement as an enormous, unified force that will, like a cresting tide, sweep the old order away. Still, in this age of climate change and neoliberal budgets, it's a matter of life and death that we seize every opportunity to organize together across and in spite of our differences. As Schofield observes, "The effects of austerity are a significant challenge. Sometimes it feels like cuts are coming faster than we can mobilize to fight back, especially when it comes to services for the poor."

Perhaps an altogether different metaphor is required to reflect today's feminisms. Thinking of feminist science fiction writer Ursula Le Guin's wonderful novella *The Word for World is Forest*, it occurs to me, listening to these five feminists, that a more useful analogy for today's feminisms might be forests rather than waves. From saplings to tall trees, the forest is a place where symbiosis rules, where organisms are mutually interdependent, and where diversity, not monoculture, is the stuff of life. Such a metaphor might be more in line with the ways in which people currently doing feminist work create alliances and build coalitions with those formerly assumed to have little in common with each other.

Today's feminisms, deeply rooted and ever-growing, are breathing fresh air into the lungs of the world through diverse modes of gender-based organizing – such as Indigenous allyship, sex worker struggles, and trans activism – that address deeply painful and challenging fault lines in historical feminist movements. In our feminist forests, we cannot escape the knowledge of our interdependence, for our very survival depends upon it. In these lush thickets of feminism, my canopy is your shade, your roots are my support, and together we must find ways to allow all of us to grow.

1. Do you think framing the history of feminism in terms of "waves" is helpful? Or is this reductive? Explain your answer.

2. Do you agree with Dilani Mohan that the so-called "call-out culture" is silencing those who might otherwise contribute to ongoing dialogue about feminism? Why or why not?

"FEMINISM'S WHITE DEFAULT," BY NORA LORETA, FROM *BRIARPATCH*, APRIL 18, 2016

In the hotel bar at the aging Winnipeg airport, about a dozen of us waited for delayed flights to carry us to destinations farther east. It was 2011 and we had just survived RebELLEs, a conference for young feminists.

The conference collapsed after a series of crises, the most explosive of which was the abject failure of the conference organizers and most delegates to confront white supremacy. This was underscored by a women of colour caucus filled mostly with white women wanting to learn about racism, and debates among white women about who is more colonized in Canada (Quebecers vs. Indigenous peoples). As a result, the second of what many hoped would be a triennial event ended with hundreds of women crying. It would not be attempted again.

It was Tria Donaldson's first experience with the feminist movement. Going to RebELLEs was supposed to be an opportunity to explore feminism and feminist organizing. As an organizer in Victoria, she had mostly been involved in environmental justice and anti-racist movements. As a young woman of Punjabi and Mohawk descent, she was excited to go to the conference and be among women who looked like her. Despite being accustomed to entering spaces that she describes as "fairly white," this conference surpassed even that expectation. "It was brutal," she says.

Donaldson, now a union activist based in Regina, remains critical of how the conference was organized: "I think [RebELLEs] was indicative of where mainstream feminism is right now, but it is also where a lot of our movements are. There's lip service paid to racism and there's not a lot of intersectionality."

THE FEMINIST CRITIQUE

Syreeta Neal, a Black-mixed womanist, wouldn't call herself a feminist: "It doesn't feel like it's a space that's inclusive or intersectional enough right now for me to feel like I'm a part of it."

The lack of intersectionality within the feminist movement remains the biggest challenge to its legitimacy. North America was built on white supremacy, the more realistic description of what many people call white privilege. Economic and social policies have advanced white people at the expense of nonwhite people since contact: from free land offers to European immigrants to the genocidal policies used to attack Indigenous peoples, our histories have built the Canada we experience today, and racism is woven into all of society's structures.

Part of these structures includes the normalization of our hetero-patriarchal system, which marginalizes and dehumanizes queer and trans folks, and assumes that the heterosexual nuclear family, led by a man, is the most legitimate unit of Canadian society.

By default, this extends to women's collective identity. Whiteness is normalized, generalized, and is assumed to be the face of the average woman. White feminists have, by and large, failed to confront the structures that maintain and promote white supremacy. As a result, they continue to organize in ways that reproduce these systems of oppression in the feminist movement itself.

Ruth Koleszar-Green, a professor of social work at York University, argues that the very foundations of Western feminism are part of the problem. As a social movement rooted in the European history of women's liberation from being the property of white men, in its current orientation it can't properly reflect the historical or ongoing experiences of colonization.

"Feminism wants to tell me what it means to be a woman, which becomes a colonial discourse, instead of looking at what I am, or who I am, as a Mohawk woman. And those identities cannot be separated," says Koleszar-Green.

"For me, it's still the fact that feminism 'saves Indians,'" she says. And if it's not trying to save them, feminism often pays lip service to Indigenous women but rarely asks for them to speak up: "We're put on the stage ... as Aboriginal women we're asked to smudge, say our prayer, and then asked to leave the stage ... or when the Elder takes the stage and speaks and people get frustrated about how long the Elder takes ... feminism does it over and over and over again."

"It's rare to have movements led by people of colour unless it's a marginalized movement, like [the one for] murdered and missing Indigenous women," says Donaldson. She argues that even in situations where it should be obvious for feminist organizations to take on certain campaigns, they often simply aren't there. She points to the crisis of forced sterilization of Indigenous people in Saskatoon as one example, where the reproductive justice movement has failed to meaningfully organize against this ongoing practice.

"The conquering of the Earth, land, people, and all that lives on the planet in the name of wealth, progress, industrialization, and capitalism has always been intertwined. Part of the rage that Indigenous and racialized women have with white women is that white women often only wanted the same benefits from the system as white men, but have not wanted to radically change the system the way that Indigenous and racialized women would have wanted," says Tina Lopes, a facilitator who works with organizations to bring about systemic change.

Lopes contends that the challenge to resist white-centric feminism, "has existed from the time that white women started gathering to fight for rights. Racialized and Indigenous women would have always known in our bodies that what was happening to us as women was an extension of what would then be used to justify the way that our people were being treated and the land was being exploited."

"SILENCING IS VIOLENCING"

White supremacy is maintained in progressive spaces by rendering diverse voices invisible. Koleszar-Green is often frustrated by how she sees Indigenous women treated in feminist spaces – similar to how men treat women under patriarchy. "I'm told over and over and over again that I'm just a colonial body: I'm disposable and if I'm visible, I should become good chattel,' seen and not heard, speak when spoken to and so on. That perpetuation of how structures have been built causes a constant picking at how colonization has attempted to erase and eradicate."

"Women in Canada who are racialized, who are Indigenous, don't want to work with myopic white women who have not learned from years and years of history and examples that tell us: 'here's how to do it wrong,"' says Sandy Hudson, a co-founder of Black Lives Matter-Toronto. She notes that while it's critical to centre the most marginalized groups in progressive campaigns, there's also a very important strategic reason to do this.

"We miss huge opportunities for movement building ... and what are we helping to perpetuate? In not organizing in these strategic ways, we are perpetuating different kinds of ways that sexism impacts different types of work," says Hudson. She asks why feminists refer to the $0.73 wage gap rather than fighting to close the much larger gap between white men and racialized women. Not only do those women need relief the most – as they only make 55.6 per cent of white men's wages, on average – but the campaign would be more compelling if women were to identify just how much further ahead white men really are.

DISMANTLING WHITE SUPREMACY IN FEMINISM

The truth on which feminism is built – that radical social change can only be achieved through solidarity – remains central, even if mainstream feminism has failed to embody this. For Donaldson, success will be connected to how feminists confront the forces that seek to uphold gender inequality: "The systems that oppress us work best when we're divided. Movements haven't been very good [at finding] ways to meaningfully bring folks from other perspectives within their movement. How much stronger would we be if we were actually able to elevate marginalized voices in a meaningful way?"

"White women should be expected to confront white supremacy. Women of colour can scream about this ... but until the people who have a seat at the table start flipping tables and making a commotion, there's only so much we can do from outside of the house," says Neal.

To do this, activists need to form meaningful relationships with each other: "The most important thing is to work with community. If you don't have that human connection to somebody, it's really hard for people to care on an emotional level," says Neal.

Lopes asserts that part of what is needed to confront white supremacy in feminism is "to actually change the way in which our organizations, institutions and society confers-opportunities and the various beneficial aspects of society. There have been gains made by white women that have not been afforded to Indigenous and racialized women."

Movements led by women, like Idle No More, demonstrate the critical importance of centring non-white voices in social movements – social change is impossible unless we confront the layered experiences of oppression within Canadian society.

Black Lives Matter likewise has intentionally placed the most marginalized voices at the centre of their organizing efforts: "Transfeminism is at the core ... [which] came to be thanks to the queer Black women who are rooted in a transfeminist politic. We want to ensure that our politics work for the people most affected by white supremacy and anti-Black racism, in the most urgent way," says Hudson.

"If we don't work from there, we'll always leave people out. Our history shows us that. We study our history and try to learn from where we feel like movements in the past could have been stronger. It's been extremely powerful to be that type of organization and to be engaging academics and non-academics, teachers and parents, and trans folks, gender non-conforming folks, and everyone that makes up the Black community."

"We're defining ourselves and defining resistance the way it should be defined" – an important piece of wisdom for feminists everywhere.

1. Do you see white supremacy as the primary problem with mainstream feminism?

2. According to the author, how might centering indigenous and non-white voices within feminism enrich the movement?

"SHEDDING THE SUPERWOMAN MYTH," BY DEBORA L. SPAR, FROM *THE CHRONICLE OF HIGHER EDUCATION*, SEPTEMBER 2, 2013

In 2005, I was teaching a first-year class at Harvard Business School. As usual, slightly under a third of my students were women. As always, I was the only female professor.

So one evening, my female students asked me and one of my female colleagues to join them for cocktails. They ordered a lovely spread of hors d'oeuvres and white wine. They presented each of us with an elegant lavender plant.

And then, like women meeting for cocktails often do, they—well, we, actually—proceeded to complain. About how tough it was to be so constantly in the minority. About how the guys sucked up all the air around the school. About the folks in career services who told them never to wear anything but a good black pantsuit to an interview.

Over the course of the conversation, though, things began to turn. The women stopped talking about their present lives and started to focus on their futures, futures that had little to do with conferences or pantsuits and everything to do with babies, and families, and men. Most of the women were frankly intending to work "for a year or two" and then move into motherhood. These were some of the smartest and most determined young women in the country. They had Ivy League degrees, for the most part, and were in the midst of paying more than $100,000 for an M.B.A. And yet they were already deeply concerned about how they would juggle their lives, and surprisingly pessimistic about their chances of doing so.

Can women pursue their dreams without losing their sanity?

Like many women of my so-called postfeminist generation, I was raised to believe that women were finally poised to be equal with men. That after centuries of oppression, exploitation, and other bad things, women could now behave more or less the way men do. Women of my generation, growing up in the 1970s and 1980s, no longer felt we had to burn our bras in protest. Instead, with a curt nod to the bra burners who had gone before us, we could saunter directly to Victoria's Secret, buying the satin push-ups that would take us seamlessly from boardroom to bedroom and beyond.

Today, most major corporations—along with hospitals, law firms, universities, and banks—have entire units devoted to helping women (and minorities) succeed. There are diversity officers and work/family offices and gender-sensitivity training courses in all tiers of American society. The problem with these efforts is that they just don't work.

Or, more precisely, even the most well-intentioned programs to attract women or mentor women or retain women still don't deal with the basic issues that most women face. And that's because the challenges that confront women now are more subtle than those of the past, harder to recognize and thus to remove. They are challenges that stem from breast pumps and Manolo pumps, from men whose eyes linger on a woman's rear end and men who rush that same rear end too quickly out the door.

Ever since the publication of *The Feminine Mystique*, American women have been haunted by the problem of *more*. Spurred by Betty Friedan's plaintive query, "Is this all?"—inspired by feminism's struggle for expanded rights and access, seduced by Astronaut Barbie—we have stumbled into an era of towering expectations. Little girls want to be princesses. Big girls want to be superwomen. Old women want and fully expect to look young. We want more sex, more love, more jobs, more-perfect babies. The only thing we want less of, it seems, is wrinkles.

None of this, of course, can be blamed on feminism or feminists. Or, as one former radical gently reminded me recently, "We weren't fighting so that you could have Botox." Yet it was feminism that lit the spark of my generation's dreams—feminism that, ironically and unintentionally, raised the bar for women so high that mere mortals are condemned to fall below it. In its original incarnation, feminism had nothing to do with perfection. In fact, the central aim of many of its most powerful proponents was to liberate women from the unreasonable, impossible standards that had long been thrust upon them.

As feminist ideals trickled and then flowed into mainstream culture, though, they became far more fanciful, more exuberant, more trivial—something easier to sell to the millions of girls and women entranced by feminism's appeal. It is easy, in retrospect, to say that women growing up in that world should have seen through the fantasy to the underlying struggle, that they—we— should have realized the myths of Charlie (both the angels and the perfume) and fought from the outset for the real rights of women. But most of us didn't, not because we were foolish, necessarily, but because it's hard, coming of age, to embrace the struggles of your parents' generation. And so we embraced the myth instead, planning, like Atalanta, to run as fast as the wind and choose the lives we wanted.

Meanwhile, none of society's earlier expectations of women disappeared. The result is a force field of highly unrealistic expectations. A woman cannot work a 60-hour week in a high-stress job and be the same kind of parent she would have been without that job and all the stress. And she cannot save the world and look forever like a 17-year-old model.

No man can do that, either; no human can. Yet women are repeatedly berating themselves for failing at this kind of balancing act, and (quietly, invidiously) berating others when something inevitably slips. Think of the schadenfreude that erupts every time a high-profile woman hits a bump in either her career or her family life. Poor Condoleezza Rice, left without a boyfriend. Sloppy Hillary, whose hair is wrong again. Bad Marissa Mayer, who dared announce her impending pregnancy the same week she was named CEO of Yahoo. She could not pull it off (snicker, snicker). She paid for her success. She. Could. Not. Do. It. All.

Because they can't possibly be all things at once, women are retreating to the only place they can, the only realm they have any chance of actually controlling. Themselves.

Rather than focusing on the external goals that might once have united them, women are micromanaging the corners of their lives and, to a somewhat lesser extent, those of their children. Think about it: How many stories will you find in women's magazines about the pursuit of anything other than bodily or familial perfection?

To be sure, this turn to the personal is not restricted to women. It follows a trajectory that can be traced back to Woodstock, or, more precisely, to the jagged route that befell the members of the Me Generation. Along the way, the struggle for individual liberties was transformed into the mantle of individualism.

Just as Reagan and Thatcher led the fight to privatize markets, so, too, have women raised since the 1960s led the charge to privatize feminism. It's not that we're against feminism's ideals. Indeed, younger women are (not surprisingly) far more likely to be in the work force than were their mothers. Younger women are wholeheartedly devoted to birth control and to sexual freedom. They account for a majority of this country's college students and a growing chunk of its professional class. Sixty-six percent of mothers with children younger than 17 work outside the home.

Yet because these women are grappling with so many expectations—because they are struggling more than they care to admit with the sea of choices that now confronts them—most of them are devoting whatever energies they have to controlling whatever is closest to them. Their kids' homework, for example. Their firm's diversity program. Their weight.

My generation made a mistake. We took the struggles and the victories of feminism and interpreted them somehow as a pathway to personal perfection. We privatized feminism and focused only on our dreams and our own inevitable frustrations. Feminism was supposed to be about granting women power and equality, and then about harnessing that power for positive change. Younger generations of women have largely turned away from those external, social goals.

So what, then, do we do?

Two generations after *Roe v. Wade*, two generations after Title IX and sexual liberation, we are still circling around the same maddening questions. Can women really have it all? Is there another way, a real way, for women to balance their personal and professional lives? Can the lofty aspirations of the early feminists—for equality, opportunity, choice—be meshed with their daughters' stubborn yearning for more-traditional pleasures, like white weddings and monogamy? And can women pursue their dreams—all their dreams—without losing their sanity?

Yes, I would argue, they can. But not along completely gender-blind lines. We need a revised and somewhat reluctant feminism, one that desperately wishes we no longer needed a women's movement but acknowledges that we still do. A feminism based at least in part on difference.

Women need to realize that having it all means giving something up—choosing which piece of the perfect picture to relinquish, or rework, or delay.

Women, in other words, are not perfect. And they are not identical to men. They are physical and social beings, marked by flaws, programmed to reproduce, destined to age, and generally inclined to love. Any approach to women's issues must start from the reality of women's lives rather than from an idealized or ideological view of who they should be and what they should want. This does not in any way mean that women should lower their sights or accept anything less than total equality with men. But it does suggest that women's paths to success may be different and more complicated than men's, and that it is better to recognize these complications than to wish them away.

To begin with, we need to recognize that biology matters. Women are not in any way physically inferior to men, but they are distinctly and physically different. They have wombs and breasts and ovaries, physiological attributes that—for better or for worse—tend to affect the course of their lives. Feminism, for many good reasons, has tended to downplay these physical differences.

But a new look at feminism would suggest integrating biology more explicitly, and acknowledging the not-so-subtle ways in which women's physiology can shape their destinies. Two areas are paramount: sexuality and reproduction. Although, of course, both women and men are involved in both sex and reproduction, the effects fall differently on women.

Let's start with sex. Most women—not all, but most—approach sexual relations differently than men do. They are more interested in romantic entanglements than casual affairs, and more inclined to seek solace in relationships. Biologically, these preferences make sense, since it is women who benefit reproductively from relationships that extend beyond the moment of conception. Sociologically, though, they set the stage for an awful lot of workplace complications. If men and women are working together, some subset of them are liable to get involved in sexual encounters. For men—in general—the focus of those encounters is likely to be purely sexual. For women—in general, again — there is more of an emphasis on, or at least desire for, a relationship. Right from the outset, then, this imbalance puts women at a disadvantage.

To deal with those admittedly awkward possibilities, most organizations have enforced strict relationship policies over the past few decades. At some level, these restrictions make sense. But they don't help women. In fact, by rigidly drawing attention to the perils of sexual attraction, they can drive men away from the kind of relationships that would help women advance—the kind of relationships that senior men regularly have with junior men. I will always recall a conversation with a senior executive who openly joked that he would never take a woman on a consulting trip. "My wife would kill me!" he said. "And so," I muttered under my breath, "your wife is happy, but you'll never promote a deserving woman."

The way out of this mess is complicated but relatively clear. Organizations must be vigilant in promoting policies against sexual harassment. At the same time, though, they should be less puritanical about the possibilities of sex and sexual attraction. Because if all attraction constitutes harassment, and all relationships are marked by fear, then women will constantly be at a disadvantage.

The other physical difference that separates men from women is the act of reproduction. Having babies shapes women's lives in ways that have barely been touched by the otherwise significant social changes of the past 50 years. Before women have children, they can compete fairly evenly across most segments of life. They can play sports and be educated and gain access to nearly every job or profession. These are the victories that feminism has wrought.

After women have children, however, the lines of their lives begin to depart from men's. Even if they are lucky enough to have decent maternity leaves and good child care, women quickly find themselves pumping breast milk at the office and lumbering under the effects of too many sleep-deprived nights. They dodge meetings to make doctor's appointments and suffer an onslaught of guilt every time they leave a crying child to attend a conference. These aspects of mothering defy government regulation and corporate policy; these are the pulls that feminism forgot. And they are not going away.

To deal with such tensions successfully, therefore, women (and men) need to be far more explicit about recognizing the specific dilemmas of motherhood. Yes, companies can and should strive to create generous maternity leaves and family-friendly workplaces. Yes, governments should aim to provide more accessible and affordable child care.

But at the end of the day, women who juggle children and jobs will still face a serious set of tensions that simply don't confront either men (except in very rare cases) or women who remain childless. Women cannot avoid those tensions entirely, but they can make choices. They can choose, for instance, between high-paying jobs in far-off cities and lower-paying ones that might leave them closer to family and friends willing to help with the predictable crises of child rearing. They can choose careers with more or less flexibility, and husbands with more or less interest in shouldering child-care responsibilities. The point is that women need to make these choices and realize their impact rather than simply hope for the best.

Which brings me to the second category of things we can do to deal with the proverbial "women's problem." We can begin to redefine the meaning of choice.

For decades now, ever since the passage of *Roe v. Wade*, the word "choice" has been linked inextricably to the goal of giving women control over their bodies and reproductive rights. Those are vitally important concerns. But choice itself is a much bigger concept and needs to be understood by women in all its complexity. Today, women in the United States enjoy options that would have confounded their ancestors. They can get married, or not; have children, or not; pursue a profession, or not. They can choose the shape of their noses, the level of their education, the religion of their partner—even, if they want, the musical talents of their child's egg donor. The problem, though, is that this multitude of choices can feel overwhelming.

The problem is not hard to fix. In theory, at least, it demands little more than a change in attitude, a societal ratcheting down of the great expectations that now engulf women. Women need to realize that having it all means giving something up—choosing which piece of the perfect picture to relinquish, or rework, or delay.

If women are ever to solve the "women's problem," they also need to acknowledge that they can't, and shouldn't, do it alone. Men must help.

Both genders need to be more forthright in discussing the obstacles that women face. All too often, women are scared of raising the topic of gender with men, thinking it will brand them as radicals or troublemakers, while men are terrified of saying or doing anything that might classify them as politically incorrect. The result is that no one says anything productive at all.

Finally, it is crucial to remember whence we came. Feminism was never supposed to be a 12-step program toward personal perfection. It's time now to go back, to channel the passion of our political foremothers and put it again to good use. We need to focus less of our energies on our own kids' SAT scores and more on fighting for better public schools; less time on competitive cupcake-baking and more on supporting those few brave women willing to run for office. We need fewer individual good works and more collective efforts.

Feminism already taught us how to organize, how to agitate, how to petition for things like equal pay and better incentives for child care. We—the women born after feminism's rise, the women who may have discarded or disdained it—ought to get back on that wheel and figure out how to make it work. Moreover, and with the benefits of 50 years behind us, we can also move to what might be considered a softer and gentler form of feminism, one less invested in proving women's equality (since that battle has more or less been won) and less upset with men.

Which brings me to my last point. The feminism that I recall was supposed to be joyous. It was about expanding women's choices, not constraining them. About making women's lives richer and more fulfilling. About freeing their sexuality and the range of their loves.

There was pain and sweat along the way, but the end point was idyllic, liberating women—liberating them—from the pains of the past and the present. Somewhere, though, the joy fell out of that equation, along with the satisfaction that true choice should bring. If women want to work in high-powered jobs, they should. If they want to work part time, or from home, or not at all if they can afford it, that's perfectly all right, too. If they don't want to be neurosurgeons or look like Barbie or hook up every weekend because it doesn't give them pleasure, they should consciously and explicitly hold back, choosing not to indulge other people's preferences. If they like to bake elaborate organic cupcakes, they should. And if they don't, they should send Ring Dings to the bake sale and try not to feel guilty.

We need to struggle. We need to organize. And we need to dance with joy.

1. The author claims that women are "physical and social beings, marked by flaws, programmed to reproduce, destined to age, and generally inclined to love." Do you find anything problematic about this sentence? If so, what?

2. This article urges women to turn away form individualism and focus on collective goals. Is the tone of this article in harmony with this message, in your opinion?

"CALLING ALL MEN – FIVE WAYS YOU CAN BE A FEMINIST AT WORK," BY SCOTT TAYLOR, FROM *THE CONVERSATION* WITH THE PARTNERSHIP OF THE UNIVERSITY OF BIRMINGHAM, AUGUST 2, 2016

Is the need for feminism dead? Saatchi & Saatchi boss Kevin Roberts seems to think so, at least in the advertising industry. He's been put on leave for saying the gender equality debate in his industry is "over". So at least one senior executive disagrees. Cindy Gallop, former president of global advertising agency Bartle Bogle Hegarty in New York, meanwhile, has recently described advertising as: "a closed loop of white guys talking to other white guys about other white guys."

Robert's comments – which provoked much criticism – are especially puzzling when so many high profile men are declaring themselves to be feminists. When Canada's prime minister Justin Trudeau formed a cabinet last year that was 50% women, he was asked why he'd made that decision. "Because it's 2015," he replied. Both Trudeau and US president, Barack Obama, have declared themselves to be proud feminists.

But sexism and sexist discrimination still happens in every workplace, every day, and it's mostly men who lead on making it happen. We can see this in terms of representation and organisational norms or practices. The numbers, still, very obviously point to the need for action – here's just are a few, for the record. In the City of London 41% employees are women, but only around 5% of FTSE chief executives are women; only 26% of FTSE 100 board members are women (better than 1999, admittedly, when it was 0.2%, but still far from equal).

The gender pay gap is similarly stubborn. Laura Bates, founder of the wonderful but depressing Everyday Sexism Project, is especially clear on the facts in this contentious area. Gender pay differentials start with pocket money – girls and young women paid 15% less for doing the same chores – and extends to the most prestigious professions, such as architecture – where women are paid 25% less than men. This is not dependent on education, skills, or experience – women are paid less for doing the same work as men imme-diately post-graduation, for example.

Does this make men uncomfortable? An increasing number, it seems. But if you don't have the power and authority that Trudeau or Obama have, how can you advo-cate feminism in your workplace? Here are five suggestions. Try them and see what happens – at the very least, it'll be more interesting than simply occupying the default position that many men, especially middle-class heterosexual white men, find themselves in.

1. TAKE RESPONSIBILITY FOR THE PATRIARCHY

All men at work benefit from what Australian sociologist Raewyn Connell has named the "patriarchal dividend". This is the unearned social or professional capital that men accrue, in that colleagues tend to assume men are some-how naturally more suited to being or just are better doctors, lawyers, academics, or politicians. This dividend doesn't just happen – it has to be reproduced and maintained for future generations. If men recognise this and take responsibility for it, then we can start to make positive changes to workplaces.

2. OWN YOUR FEMINISM

Anthropologist Marjory Wolf tells us that a feminist seeks to understand and dismantle gender hierarchies in theory and practice. That's something everyone can and should do; those hierarchies don't exist for any good reason, and feminism is the best way we've found to challenge them. Make it personal – you're not speaking on behalf of women colleagues, or your female partner, or daughter – speak for yourself.

3. ACCEPT IT

Most people talk about "waves" of feminism: a first wave argued for basic property rights and the right to vote in the early 20th century; a second wave argued for equal access to education and workplaces in the 1960s; a third wave in the 1980s recognised women's experiences as varied; and we're living through a social media-enabled fourth wave now.

It's time we accepted that feminism is necessary – and probably always will be. British sociologist Sylvia Walby prefers the metaphor of a "spiral", because it makes clear that positive change is happening, and because it also tells us that we're continually dealing with the same thing – irrational discrimination based on gender identity.

4. SPEAK OUT

One of the most feminist acts that a man can take in the workplace is to say something. It doesn't have to be complex or long-winded – two of the easiest things to say are "that's sexist" or "that's discriminatory". At the moment, a man's voice is more likely to be heard through the background noise of the average workplace – so use it to call out actions, behaviour, or ways of working that are sexist.

5. ACT

Finally, act in ways that make a real difference. Many selection panels are put together with an eye to "equality" by including one woman, often on a panel of five or more people. That's not equality – it's what Harvard academic Rosabeth Moss Kanter identified in the 1970s as tokenism. All the research we have about gender dynamics in teams and groups tells us, very clearly, that change is only achieved when women are at least one third of the group by number. Why not aim for 50%? That's equality.

There's so many other things men can say, do, or make happen, to change the numbers and to start to change workplace cultures that support the dominant masculinities that benefit such a small number of blokes. Some are apparently trivial – purposely including women in group conversations, for example, where men often overlook or talk over women.

And some of them are apparently more significant. "Leaning out", for example, is a way that men can make space for women to move into the positions of power and authority that they deserve or have earned, but are excluded from. Above all, men have to recognise that practising feminism is not difficult – you just have to decide to do it. And it'll make workplaces better for all of us.

1. Do you think it's possible for men to "do feminism"? Are there any problems with this?

2. What are some reasons why advocating feminism might benefit men as well as women?

"LITERATURE, PATRIARCHY, AND PLATH," BY SARAH RUDEN, FROM THE *NATIONAL REVIEW*, AUGUST 10, 2015

Perhaps the best-known literary feminist cri de coeur is Virginia Woolf's *A Room of One's Own* (1929), which lamented women's dependent state and projected that female writers, granted education, personal space, and independent income, would give the men a run for their money. In thousands of fem-lit and women's-studies classes, Woolf's hindsight dramatization of what would have happened to Shakespeare's equally talented sister has overshadowed the essay's utter failure as prophecy.

Jane Austen, who died in 1817, would likely poll as the greatest woman writer. In *A Room*, Woolf cites Austen's self-effacing secretiveness while writing, though in the parlor amid callers and servants coming and going. In another extended essay, *Three Guineas* (1938), Woolf lists the desiderata for the nurture of women's minds as "travel, society, solitude, a lodging apart from the family house."

But the spread of traditional (and, by the way, elite) masculine prerogatives to millions of women, though it has produced many social goods, has not yet resulted in feminine literary achievement of Austen's quality. This is a hugely interesting fact to look at as it tosses among the various waves of feminism, a movement that barely existed in the England of Austen's lifetime; the French Revolution had hyped but in practice discredited feminism, and the drive for women's legal and political rights that grew up as a little sister to Abolitionism (in religious rather than artsy circles, and primarily in America) wasn't dreamed of in the Steventon rectory.

But there Austen's expressiveness flourished, hardly choked off by ignorance and frustration, but rather a model of balance and humanity. Call me an outrageous partisan, but I don't think that any man, whatever his practical advantages, ever wrote more perfectly.

I wonder whether Austen sprang up in a historical sweet spot, after a female literary calling stopped being an absurdity but before social and financial support from male relatives stopped being a moral obligation. If so, what does that say of the tornado of changing women's roles that hit Sylvia Plath, perhaps the most talented 20th-century woman poet?

Most of Plath's work played frantically to literary fashions, and she exhausted herself with efforts at elaborate private and public women's roles: submissive good-girl student, Seven Sisters candidate for Ivy League chatelaine, glamour-mag fiction impresario, glamour puss and seductress—but most strenuously, nurturing wife and mother, and supportive daughter of an ailing, overstressed widow. Her truest voice was one of despair, in the months before her suicide at only 30. To me, what seems to have been most tragically lacking for her was not freedom or opportunity, but patriarchal "oppression" and "condescension."

With her schedule under fatherly supervision, she would have felt more in control of her energy's uses, in the usual way of the well brought up. Restricted in dating, she would not have marketed herself through sex, a ludicrous strategy (but apparently the best she could come up with) for a woman on her own seeking a marriage that would, effectively, sponsor her writing. Doing the dishes and being polite to family friends, she would not have run back and forth between self-mythologizing and self-hatred.

Her contemporary Flannery O'Connor, a shockingly good fiction writer, got the better of isolation and confinement (illness kept her living at home with her widowed mother for her last 14 years) because she was a devout Catholic. Her life's social and emotional possibilities being well defined from the start, she didn't have to invent them, but could concentrate on exploring new kinds of writing.

In my experience, women are tough cookies. I have no basis for suspecting that they're more feeble at life-invention than men would be; but certainly during the last century most women were left with an outrageous amount of life invention to do, which could well have reduced psychic resources for literary invention. Sylvia Plath's life and work seem to exemplify this rather pathetically.

Plath was born in 1932 and lost her professor father—who had been immensely proud of her precocity—in 1940. Her mother's entry into the work force was part of a nationwide movement: Vast numbers of women with children, in the absence of their men, took industrial jobs in support of the war.

That work didn't entail all the exhilaration today's media like to depict shows in their reaction when the war ended: Hardly any fought to keep "men's" jobs. Most bought into the religion of domesticity and the female image: a smiling, slim, beautifully coiffed, brightly clad woman, mopping or baking daintily, was the surety for the world being under control, the good life being possible.

This was the attitude that greeted Plath post-war, during her teens. A few professional women, however, would be mentors, were there, too, reacting against this attitude and demanding a brilliant girl's deference; Plath was irritated at them and nervous about the suburbs by turns. She struggled with questions of vocation and romance to the degree that her first suicide attempt came after her prize guest-editorship at *Mademoiselle* magazine and her emergence from scholarship-girl awkwardness into beauty and charisma that made dozens of conventionally eligible men available to her.

It's fascinating to speculate about what Virginia Woolf would have thought of *The Bell Jar* (1963), Plath's lightly fictionalized account of her breakdown in the fast lane. The book suggests the kind of "novel of silence" Woolf herself wrote, drawing on the typical inwardness of female experience. Plath's first-person protagonist is poor, provincial, and naive, and must struggle within a narrow space—mostly an internal one.

But far from the polite hush of the drawing room, *The Bell Jar's* Esther Greenwood is out there, her future constantly and indifferently at play, like a lottery ball ricocheting among countless others in a glass box in a TV studio. The surface of the novel is bright and shallow, like the Technicolor football romance Esther watches among the other guest editors, while an attack of ptomaine poisoning starts (the germs having been hidden in the ravishing-looking crab salad of a gala lunch). But every image is memorable, attached as it is to the relentless grief of the intuitive speaker. She has no father to guide her through the treasures and the trash, and no religion to turn to; her mother pooh-poohs her draw toward Catholicism.

Toward the end of Plath's life, in her loneliness and fear as her marriage and professional contacts deteriorated, her words centered on the exalted meaninglessness of the world into which she had been thrown—or, rather, the world that could be given meaning only through her own words. She was like a lynx hunting, her achievement a sort of apotheosis of nature writing. These lines are from her poem "Elm," in the posthumously published collection *Ariel*:

Love is a shadow.

How you lie and cry after it.

Listen: these are its hooves: it has gone

    off, like a horse.

All night I shall gallop thus, impetuously,

Till your head is a stone, your pillow a

    little turf,

Echoing, echoing.

Ariel exists because Plath's husband, the poet Ted Hughes, his rights over Plath's literary estate still intact (because they were not yet divorced at the time of her death), and his appreciation of Plath's genius (and its earning potential) undiminished by an excruciating breakup, published intelligently from her hoard of manuscripts. He also selectively destroyed and edited to save himself and the children embarrassment.

The Second Wave, equal-opportunity feminism of the Sixties and Seventies was both a magical chance and a curse for Plath's reputation. Hordes of us young women were feeling stifled and unappreciated despite our supposed giftedness, and so identified manically with her. I once found that a previous reader—female, I'm certain—had, in a transgressively Plathian manner, annotated a library copy of *The Bell Jar*. For example, in the margin beside the place where Esther meets a marriage proposal worded "How would you like to be Mrs. Buddy Willard?" with "an awful impulse to laugh," my predecessor had written, "Me too."

Plath's poems, however, were relatively unpopular. We could sort of imagine writing something like *The Bell Jar*. (Lots of us tried.) But the poetry was another matter. I think it didn't appeal to us because it was too good, beyond any conceivable aspirations of our own. *The Bell Jar* itself testifies to the bell curve. There are very few women geniuses, which is one reason society doesn't easily accommodate them.

The Third Wave of feminism was perhaps less about male backlash than about female backtracking, out of embarrassment at the Second Wave's unrealizable projections. Women weren't, as a class, achieving on a professional level with men, and the excuses of disadvantage wore away as opportunities grew. So why not just glorify the ordinariness of women, as lovers, mothers, quilters, gardeners, authors in search of their mothers' gardens, etc.?

For a striking female achiever like Plath, the cost to status was pitiful. From the late Seventies, the thrust of her treatment turned from excoriation of Ted Hughes as an envious "killer" of his intimate literary rival to, on the one hand, the celebration of Plath as earth mother or girl next door (virtually ourselves!), and on the other, the scarifying of her as an evil, unnatural woman (so that it was better for us to be ordinary).

Trapped in the most reductive terms of her gender, used like any fantasy-laden image for easy ego-gratification, she made Jane Austen look like a free spirit. The radical politics of envy, forcible leveling, and arbitrary redistribution had effected a terrible irony: Plath's work, evincing unique insight and eloquence, was neglected, but her ordinary virtues were smarmily commended and her ordinary failings haughtily sniffed at, like those of an absent neighbor by a merciless coffee klatch.

I encountered the Plath memory wars in literary magazines in the mid Nineties, and I documented several major skirmishes at the end of the decade for a Johns Hopkins Writing Seminars biography course. Plath was the ideal daughter; she was spoiled from the get-go. Plath was a saintly wife; she was an impossible, self-immolating wife. Plath was a lunatic; she was as normal as they come. Plath was a delightful guest/host/room-mate/ friend; she was infuriating.

Jane Austen's memory has enjoyed one of the sublime gifts of patriarchy: her family's insistence on guarding her personal reputation. Her sister destroyed all the letters Austen would have minded posterity's seeing. Other relatives wrote warmhearted memoirs. Now, the data age brings extremes of prying into and trivializing writers. It's worse for a significant woman writer, her less familiar public presence being confused and mashed up with her private life. That shows contempt, of course, for her intricate toil in creating a special persona for the public. Once considered her legitimate job, or even her decorous duty, now this is supposed to be a withholding, a sham, like prissy chastity.

Over time, what are essentially attempts to compete with Plath in telling her story have become rather surreal. Chroniclers must think their own sheer insistent presence—as if on personal blogs—has to win out. Elizabeth Winder's *Pain, Parties, Work: Sylvia Plath in New York, Summer 1953* (2013) redepicts the single month Plath spent at *Mademoiselle*, as if *The Bell Jar*'s opening chapters were inadequate. Elizabeth Sigmund's *Sylvia Plath in Devon: A Year's Turning* (2015) reminisces about a period—deemed vital because Sigmund was present?— of work on *The Bell Jar* and the *Ariel* poems. Shut up and read those books, Plath shouts from the grave.

Andrew Wilson's *Mad Girl's Love Song: Sylvia Plath and Life before Ted* (2013) rebels against Hughes's influence on her reputation, only to hand her over to (among countless others) a simultaneous interpreter complaining that she failed to admire his costly vicuna bedspread on her single, uneventful visit to his apartment, and a female acquaintance professing to have lost interest in Plath when first meeting her owing to a breach of table manners.

Is one lesson of Plath's reception that we lack the detachment, the contemplative capacity even to read significant literary work on its own? And are we, under a thin political gloss of sympathy with the struggles of talented women, too mean-spirited and narcissistic to either support and commend them or let them alone?

1. What broad points about feminism can we take away from these insights into the public personas and private lives of Sylvia Plath and Jane Austen?

2. The author suggests that objective literary criticism of female genius is difficult due to envy or narcissism. Do you agree with this? Why or why not?

CHAPTER 2

WHAT THE GOVERNMENT AND POLITICIANS SAY

In 2016, Hillary Clinton came close to winning the presidency of the United States before losing to Republican candidate Donald Trump. Though Clinton is the first woman in the nation's history to run at the top of a major party ticket, she is not the first woman to run for president. That distinction belongs to Victoria Woodhull, the Equal Rights Party presidential nominee in 1872. Long ago, Woodhull ran on a platform advocating contraception, abortion, and marriage (or divorce) on women's terms. Woodhull did not win. In fact, Woodhull could not even vote. It was not until the passage of the Nineteenth Amendment in 1919 that women would finally gain the right to vote, well into the women's suffrage movement by many decades.

That almost a century and half after Woodhull's unsuccessful presidential bid, Hillary Clinton's platform necessarily included basic reproductive rights for women indicates how little lasting progress we have made with respect to women's political and personal rights. Since 2011, over 200 new restrictions on abortion have been proposed. This is part of a concerted effort by Republican lawmakers to push back against *Roe v. Wade*. Under the auspices of protecting women, laws such as Targeted Restrictions of Abortion Providers (TRAP) impose onerous and expensive conditions on abortion clinics, with the barely concealed aim of shutting their doors when they can't comply. Below, Victoria A. Brownworth situates this legislation as part of what she identifies as a war against women in America.

Others found Clinton a troubling candidate because of her hawkish foreign policy, close corporate ties, and use of racially insensitive terms like "super predator." As Peter Bloom argues, Clinton was indisputably a highly qualified presidential candidate. A victory for her would have shattered the glass ceiling that has prevented women from holding the highest office in the land, no doubt an inspirational prospect for all women, but especially young women. On the other hand, that a woman must espouse many status quo values (to say nothing of being the former first lady) compromises her feminist credentials somewhat. For this reason, Bloom contends that Clinton might be a dangerous role model.

By simply looking to Europe, we find many female leaders such as German Chancellor Angela Merkel. Recently, the government of Sweden has declared its basic alignment with feminism, the first such statement of its kind. In comparison to leading feminist nations, the US is exceptional in that so few female leaders have broken through, and so much work must be done to protect basic freedom and rights for women.

"CLINTON'S INSPIRING AND TROUBLING LIBERAL FEMINISM," BY PETER BLOOM, FROM *COMMON DREAMS*, AUGUST 2, 2016

In the first time in its 240 year history, the United States has a female nominee for President in one of its major political parties. Hillary Clinton's nomination is clearly a landmark moment in American history. It represents a public blow to a traditionally male dominated political system and possibly beyond.

This inspiring victory, however, is also quite unsettling. It links feminism to a candidate with a troubling legacy of militarism, economic elitism and social Conservatism. Even more worrying, is the popular use of feminism to justify this record – as it is argued that for Clinton to be successful she had to be willing to "compromise" her values.

Clinton's victory reflects competing and both justifiable sentiments. It is sexist and unacceptable to dismiss how inspiring and empowering it has been for women as well as men. Yet its explicit and implicit legitimization of the negative impact she has had on people— including women—in the US and globally as a corporate lawyer and public official perpetuates a troubling brand of contemporary feminism.

AN INSPIRING VICTORY

Following an intensely contested primary, Hillary Clinton has officially accepted the Democratic nomination for President. Her victory prompted a wave of popular reflection on the significance of this victory. It highlights the potential for progress in America—as the beginning of the 21st century has witnessed the election of the country's first non-white President and nomination of its first female candidate.

Yet it also reveals just how unexceptional America is when it comes to combating sexism and gender discrimination. Globally, female leaders have not only broken through the glass ceiling but increasingly become the political norm. Only this month, Theresa May became the second women Prime Minister in British history. The German Angela Merkel remains one of the world's most prominent and powerful leaders. In fact females have currently assumed power in countries as wide ranging as Liberia to Croatia, Jamaica to Poland, Bangladesh to Kosovo.

Critics rightfully point to Clinton's vast racial and class privilege. She may be a woman but she is an exceedingly rich white woman. These are not advantages that can or should be easily overlooked. However, from a different perspective it is precisely this privilege that makes her nomination so extraordinary. It shows in stark detail just how patriarchal modern America remains—even for women at the very top of the social order.

Regardless of any other political differences, Hillary Clinton's victory has been inspiring. It is also setting a profoundly dangerous example for contemporary feminism and female empowerment.

A DANGEROUS ROLE MODEL

A key reason her nomination is so celebrated is that it displays to women—especially young women—that they can achieve anything. It reveals that no job, office or opportunity is closed to them due to their sex. Clinton has broken through one of the world's highest and thickest glass ceilings—creating a space for a new generation of female leaders to follow in her footsteps.

Yet it must also be asked what type of political and moral role model is she? Throughout her career she has shown a willingness to forsake seemingly any and all progressive principles for personal advantage. Whether as a member of Walmart's anti-union corporate board as first lady of Arkansas, or promoting racially charged legislation to reduce social welfare and increase mass incarceration as first lady of the United States, or championing a disastrous invasion of Iraq as a Senator or backing anti-democratic coups and dictators across the world as Secretary of State.

At the very least this is an indictment of the US system. It implies that for a woman to succeed she must be willing to embrace elitism at home and imperialism abroad. There is a certain "clear eyed" Liberal feminism that accepts and even embraces such a "Machiavellianism." Nevertheless, this realism is at direct odds with the broader tenor of Clinton's own campaign and its incessant conviction that "America is already great".

There is a worrying lesson underpinning this triumphalism, one that reflects the hyper-capitalism of the current times. In particular, it reinforces the idea that personal achievement trumps public accomplishment— that getting the job and having it on your CV is vastly more important than doing it well or using it to makes things better. It is almost besides the point that as a Senator Clinton had little legislative accomplishments— progressive or otherwise—or that as Secretary of State she authorized a record amount of arms sales while spreading the use of fracking internationally.

There is an underlying amorality to Clinton's upwardly mobile version of feminism. It is that unlike men supposedly women simply can't afford to have principles. Moreover, that having the courage of your convictions is incompatible with female success. In an era of growing inequality and authoritarianism, this makes Clinton a potentially dangerous female role model indeed.

A TROUBLING FEMINISM

The critiques of Clinton's politics should not, of course, dismiss the empowerment women and men all across the country are feeling over her nomination. It is perhaps especially difficult to remember that an event can be both justifiably inspiring and troubling when cable news and social media bombard citizens daily with facile narratives, passionately partisan perspectives and sound bites instead of deeper critical analysis. Instead of merely feting or demonizing Clinton, it is dramatically more significant to use her success as an opportunity to collectively reflect on the progress feminism has made and the struggles that still confront it.

Notably, it must be investigated which female voices are being silenced by this feminist victory. Specifically, many women of color have expressed ambivalence in relation to this event as they attempt to navigate the conflict of rejoicing in a fellow women's success while also recognizing the white privilege that enabled to Clinton while often continuing to bar their own advancement. This ambiguity is captured in the popular hashtag *#Iguessimwithher*.

Just as importantly have been the silencing of genuinely progressive female voices. They are legitimately concerned that women have actually practiced not just preached values of economic and social equality are being made invisible. As socialist councilwoman Kshama Sawant recently stated:

> A lot of people think that, well, it's a woman leader, and this is going to be important. But, look, she was on the board of Wal-Mart for six years. Wal-Mart is the world's biggest purveyor of poverty wages. And who do you think it affects? It affects women at the very bottom. You heard from the woman, the poignant story of the woman—I saw her last night at the protest—who said that because welfare was destroyed under Bill Clinton, she—her mother had to become a sex worker. Hillary Clinton was not an innocent bystander when welfare was dismantled. She actually played an active political role alongside Bill Clinton and the new Democrats. Now, as a feminist, I would have loved for her to have played an active role to shore up welfare, to make sure that women's living standards could have been improved. Unfortunately for us, she's playing a very active role as a woman, but as a defender of Wall Street.

Fundamentally, Clinton's triumph critically raises new questions for American feminism. Is it possible to create a politics of gender equality that also challenges the capitalism and modern day colonialism that is so destructive to the life of women in the United States and globally? Must motivated women accept the need for having "dirty hands" in a corrupt system or can they use their power to fight for a less "dirty" feminism and world?

Undeniably the nomination of Hillary Clinton is a historic and landmark event for the country. The hope is that the next female nominee for President is less politically and morally troubling.

1. According to the author, Clinton's presidential nomination was bittersweet, due to her compromised record as a progressive. Do you agree that Clinton represents an amoral version of feminism?

2. Do you think it's possible for mainstream female leaders to challenge capitalism and imperialism? Or is gender equity only possible within a hegemonic value system?

"WHO IS WINNING THE WAR ON WOMEN?: WOMEN'S HISTORY MONTH IS THE TIME TO REFLECT ON OUR LACK OF PROGRESS," BY VICTORIA A. BROWNWORTH, FROM *CURVE*, MARCH 2016

This election year, with America closer to electing a woman president than ever before, the dismissive and often derisive tone with which Women's History Month is often met feels more personal than ever.

Ted Cruz wants to spank Hillary Clinton, like he does his 5-year-old daughter. Bernie Sanders thinks Planned Parenthood and the Human Rights Campaign are as establishment as Wall Street and wants to "take them on." Marco Rubio has cosponsored several bills in the Senate limiting women's access to both contraception and abortion. Donald Trump—well, where to begin?—insinuated that Megyn Kelly was having her period when she asked him hard questions, and told Brande Roderick, "Must be a pretty picture, you dropping to your knees" in a boardroom. Jeb Bush gets confused over which is which: President Obama's older daughter, Malia, or Nobel Peace Prize-winner Malala.

Yet Oscar-winner Susan Sarandon doesn't think women should "vote with their vaginas"—as she poses on a sofa in a low-cut blouse at age 70. What year is it?

It might as well be 1872. That was the year Victoria Woodhull, a leader in the women's suffrage movement, became the first woman in America to run for president.

On Election Day 1872, Woodhull couldn't even vote for herself, because it would be another 48 years before women would get the right to vote. But as it happened, Woodhull was in prison on obscenity charges for publishing a news story about the affair between Calvinist minister and abolitionist Henry Ward Beecher and Elizabeth Tilton, the wife of his mentor, Theodore Tilton, who subsequently sued Beecher for adultery. (Beecher's siblings include Harriet Beecher Stowe, the author of *Uncle Tom's Cabin*, then the best-selling book in the world.) Woodhull published the story because Beecher preached against "free love" and was also the first president of the National Women's Suffrage Association. Woodhull wanted to expose his hypocrisy. But her news story was deemed "obscene."

Running on the ticket of the Equal Rights Party (a suffrage and abolitionist party) Woodhull was nominated to run against the incumbent, Ulysses S. Grant, a Republican, and his Democratic opponent, Horace Greeley. The Equal Rights Party (previously the People's Party) had placed noted abolitionist and freed slave Frederick Douglass on the ticket with Woodhull.

Woodhull has been described in various biographies as an iconoclast. She was 34 when she ran for president. She and her youngest sister, Tennessee (they were two of 10 children), were the first women stockbrokers and founded the first brokerage firm run by women, as well as the first newspaper run by women, *Woodhull & Claflin's Weekly*, in 1870. Woodhull's parents were illiterate and she had only a few years' schooling, but she was a prolific writer of news and essays, and the newspaper was devoted to political issues she was fervent about, including feminism.

Our first woman presidential candidate also advocated for "free love"—that is, marriage and divorce on a woman's terms. She fought for contraception and abortion rights—the same issues that presidential candidate Hillary Clinton fights for today.

Unsurprisingly, Woodhull did not fare well at the polls, receiving not a single Electoral College vote. No woman has gotten close to the presidency until now, nearly 150 years later. In 1984, Geraldine Ferraro was the first major-party vice-presidential candidate, running with Walter Mondale. They only won a single state: Minnesota. In 2008, Alaska Gov. Sarah Palin ran for vice president with Sen. John McCain. They were far more successful, winning 22 states.

The 2016 election raises the question of whether a woman president could end the war on women in America. The current presidential race has underscored the intensity of the sexism and gender apartheid still rampant in America, while the coverage of the race has resurrected every sexist trope imaginable about a woman's ability to lead.

And yet, there's no candidate in the race better equipped to be president than Hillary Clinton. Nor is there any candidate who has addressed women's issues, either in the campaign itself or in their career, like Clinton has. From her days as Arkansas' First Lady to her days as Secretary of State, Clinton has been a tireless advocate for women's rights, both at home and globally. Her speech "Women's Rights Are Human Rights"—at the 1995 United Nations Fourth World Conference on Women in Beijing—was iconic. Vital, too, in her advocacy for gender equality was Clinton's role in creating the Justice Department's Office on Violence Against Women. Clinton has also made violence against women a major part of the Clinton Foundation's Global Issues campaigns, and has focused on the sex trafficking of girls and women since her time in the Senate.

Yet, like Woodhull before her—albeit nearly 150 years apart—Clinton has been dismissed for her support of women's issues, as though they are not mainstream or important. Yet women are more than half the country. Shouldn't our issues predominate?

On the GOP side, they do. But not in a good way, as evidenced by the tack the frontrunners in the presidential race have taken on women's rights—especially reproductive rights—and on the issues of equal pay, sexual and domestic violence, immigration, and LGBT rights. It has long been true that women's rights battles and those of LGBT persons have intersected.

In early January, the National LGBTQ Task Force filed an amicus brief in the case of *Whole Women's Health v Cole*, asking the U.S. Supreme Court (SCOTUS) to "strike down draconian restrictions on abortion providers enacted by the State of Texas in 2013." If these restrictions are upheld in Texas, it would lead to the closing of all but 10 abortion clinics in the state. The brief urges the court, to carefully scrutinize the state's rationale for the law, just as SCOTUS has done with other laws that infringe upon fundamental freedoms.

"The movements for reproductive health, rights, and justice are indispensable for LGBTQ people. Our work, as repro and LGBTQ advocates, is inseparable, as we are working for the right to live our lives fully and the right to choose how we use our bodies," said Rea Carey, executive director of the National LGBTQ Task Force. "A ruling that favors discrimination under the guise of 'women's health' would negatively impact LGBTQ people."

It's hard not to get angry with celebrities who make statements like "I don't vote with my vagina"—especially when every GOP candidate for president, from the front-runners to the also-rans, have put restricting reproductive rights on their agenda. Also on their extremist agenda is overturning the SCOTUS ruling on marriage equality. What's more, the First Amendment Defense Act (FADA) has been incorporated into the Republican platform. That legislation would allow people like the now-notorious Kentucky clerk Kim Davis to violate the law in adherence to their own political or religious beliefs.

Woodhull and her sister had to publish their own newspaper in order to get their messages out. But in 2016, the news media is just as restrictive about who gives voice to issues directly related to women as it was in 1872. A January report found that men dominate the news coverage of women's reproductive issues.

"When it comes to stories about abortion and contraception, women's voices are systematically stifled—as writers and as sources," says Julie Burton, president of the Women's Media Center. Burton notes, "In articles about elections and reproductive issues, men's voices prevail, especially in coverage of presidential campaigns, with male reporters telling 67 percent of all presidential election stories related to abortion and contraception."

Gloria Steinem, co-founder of the Women's Media Center, notes, "Since women play a greater role in reproduction, it would make sense for women to be the majority of the sources and authorities in its coverage."

WMC research shows that female journalists wrote just 37 percent of articles about reproductive issues while their male counterparts wrote 52 percent. Another 11 percent did not have bylines. Quotes from men account for 41 percent of all quotes in articles about reproductive issues, while quotes from women account for just 33 percent.

Meanwhile, it's men who continue to make the decisions about our vaginas and uteruses, and it's imperative that we consider this when we vote. Every GOP candidate has decried the alleged Planned Parenthood videos—yet on Jan. 25, Texas Gov. Greg Abbott released a statement on the months long investigation. Planned Parenthood was cleared by the grand jury, but several antiabortion activists will be charged.

Attempts to restrict women's reproductive rights continue. In late January, the U.S. Supreme Court refused to allow a proposed law in North Dakota that would have made abortions illegal if a woman was more than six weeks pregnant.

That so little has changed between Woodhull, our first female presidential candidate, and our current female candidate speaks to how ingrained sexism is in America. That we are still fighting for bodily autonomy nearly a century and a half later should be shocking—yet isn't.

1. This article questions whether a female president can stop the ongoing war against women, particularly reproductive rights. What do you think?

2. Our first female presidential candidate was 150 years ago, yet the author claims we haven't come very far. Do you agree, or does this too broadly dismiss the accomplishments of second-wave feminism?

"100 YEARS OF THE 'GENDER GAP' IN AMERICAN POLITICS," BY ANYA JABOUR, FROM *THE CONVERSATION* WITH THE PARTNERSHIP OF THE UNIVERSITY OF MONTANA, NOVEMBER 24, 2016

Men and women did not vote the same way in 2016.

In fact, the Donald Trump versus Hillary Clinton contest yielded the largest gender gap – the difference between women's and men's voting behavior – in U.S. history. Clinton won women by 12 points and lost men by the same amount – a 24-point gap. The gap has grown. Twenty points separated the sexes in 2012.

Women's support was expected to help Clinton shatter "the highest glass ceiling" to become the nation's first female president.

Seeing themselves as heirs to the suffrage movement, Clinton supporters even made pilgrimages to Susan B. Anthony's grave to place their "I Voted" stickers on the suffrage leader's tombstone.

But despite garnering the most popular votes, Clinton lost in the Electoral College.

The fact that 53 percent of white women cast their ballots for Trump threatens to obscure the importance of gender to U.S. politics.

What's needed is a broader – and longer – lens.

So let's start at the beginning. How did the gender gap become so important to American politics?

WOMEN'S CLUBS AND WOMAN SUFFRAGE

My current research convinced me that the gender gap has its roots in women's political activity in the Progressive era, which began around 1880 and ran until about 1920.

During these decades of massive immigration, rapid industrialization and tremendous poverty, many Americans hoped to use the political process to address social problems in the nation's growing cities.

Women didn't yet have the right to vote, but they joined the Progressive movement by organizing clubs devoted to civic reform. The women's club movement provided millions of American women with an alternative route into the political process.

One animating issue for club women was revitalizing the campaign for female suffrage. Launched in 1848, the movement for women's voting rights had achieved only a handful of victories, all in the West, since the Civil War.

Women sought the vote for many reasons, but in turn-of-the-century America, many suffragists argued that women were ideal voters because they weren't corrupted by party politics. Instead, they argued, women were more interested in sound policies.

WOMEN'S POLITICAL CULTURE

As political outsiders, women brought a new perspective to Progressive politics. While not all women shared the same beliefs, many female activists participated in a distinctive "women's political culture."

Using their traditional domestic role to justify their unconventional political activity, many suffrage supporters argued that as "social housekeepers," women would use the vote to "clean up" both "dirty" politics and equally dirty city streets.

In addition, many "social justice feminists" saw themselves as advocates for the nation's disadvantaged and dispossessed, including women, children, workers, immigrants and African-Americans.

As a result, women made unique contributions to urban reform. For instance, in Chicago, male politicians established "red light" districts. By contrast, women activists defended the rights of accused prostitutes.

THE WOMAN'S CITY CLUB OF CHICAGO

The Woman's City Club of Chicago, while not the first or the only such organization in America, was especially important in terms of the history of women's political activism.

The club was founded in 1910 to combat the city's legendary political corruption. According to club member Louise de Koven Bowen, the organization began when a businessman told the club's first president: "I wish you women would form some kind of a club to fight our civic evils; we men have tried it and failed, perhaps you women can do something."

By waging a successful campaign giving Illinois women the right to vote in both national and local elections and encouraging women to use their votes to promote reform, the club made women a force to reckon with in electoral politics well before the adoption of the federal woman suffrage amendment in 1920.

'GOOD GOVERNMENT' AND THE GENDER GAP

In 1913, Illinois became the first state east of the Mississippi River to grant voting rights to female citizens.

Prior to the citywide elections of 1914, Chicago women's first significant voting opportunity, the Woman's City Club sponsored a massive voter registration and citizen education campaign. In addition, six women, including four club members, ran for local office.

Women voters went to the polls in high numbers, disproving skeptics' claims that women would not exercise the right to vote. Moreover, female voters consistently voted for "good government," creating one of the nation's first "gender gaps."

When the votes were counted, however, women were disappointed by the results. None of the female candidates garnered enough votes to gain office, leaving male politicians to continue business as usual. Undaunted by this setback, women activists launched a new campaign to reform Chicago politics.

THE WOMEN'S MUNICIPAL PLATFORM

In 1916, the Woman's City Club sponsored a mass meeting in downtown Chicago to protest the "spoils system" in city government and to promote progressive social policies. Women activists adopted a "Women's Municipal Platform" dedicated "to the promotion of the welfare of all the citizens and to the securing of equality of opportunity to all the children of all of the people." Club leaders demanded reforms related to public schools, health and safety, city parks and playgrounds, and the criminal justice system.

Chicago's female activists displayed a keen awareness of their distinctiveness as politically active women. According to the preamble to the platform, "women citizens" were ideal voters because they prioritized the common good over party politics.

Club women also understood their importance as pioneering female voters. The club president observed: "The attention of suffragists and anti-suffragists throughout the United States is now directed to the women of Illinois in order to determine how fully they are using their newly acquired franchise and with what results."

In fall of 1916, Chicago women turned out in impressive numbers to vote for political change.

As Progressive Party politician Charles Merriam put it in the Woman's City Club Bulletin, "What finer tribute could be paid to the intelligence of woman's vote!"

THE 'WOMEN'S VOTE' TODAY

A hundred years later, Clinton's defeat in the presidential election of 2016 indicates that despite important gains in the U.S. Senate, women in some ways remain political outsiders – but outsiders who continue to play a special role in the nation's politics.

Like Chicago club women a century before, American women activists are responding to defeat by planning a mass protest. As journalist Jill Filipovic remarks, "We fix this with more feminism, not less."

The gender gap may not have gained Clinton the presidency, but it is just as salient today as it was a century ago.

1. What were some of the reasons early feminists gave for political representation for women? What do you think of these reasons today—do they still seem credible?
2. Do you agree that women can fix what ails American politics today "with more feminism, not less"? Why or why not?

"FEMINISTS WEIGH IN ON DRAFT REGISTRATION FOR WOMEN," BY CLAIRE SCHAEFFER-DUFFY, FROM THE *NATIONAL CATHOLIC REPORTER*, JUNE 28, 2016

Recent legislative efforts to extend draft registration to young women have raised an old conundrum for some feminists. Does pursuit of gender equality include support for universal conscription?

While not all feminists are anti-militarists, opposition to war and militarism has been a strong current within the women's movement. Prominent suffragists like Quaker Alice Paul, and Barbara Deming, a feminist activist and thinker of the 1960s and 70s, were ardent pacifists. Moreover, feminist critique has often regarded the military as a hierarchical, male-dominated institution promoting destructive forms of power.

In late April, the House Armed Services Committee voted for an amendment to the national defense bill that would extend draft registration -- already a requirement for men -- to women ages 18-26. The amendment was later dropped, but in mid-June, the Senate approved a similar provision in its version of the national defense bill.

Among the amendment's staunchest defenders was Armed Services Committee member Rep. Jackie Speier (D-Calif.).

"If we want equality in this country, if we want women to be treated precisely like men are treated and that they should not be discriminated against, then we should support a universal conscription," Speier told the political website The Hill in April.

Not all feminists agree with Speier's path to equality Days after the House Armed Services Committee approved the amendment, 24-year-old Julie Mastrine, an activist and media professional, authored an online petition calling on Congress not to force women to register and instead dump the draft entirely

Mastrine, a self-described feminist libertarian, argues that draft registration violates individual choice.

"I can't imagine a more tragic loss of liberty than forcing a citizen, whether male or female, to fight in a war with which they may disagree. Equality is a moot point if personal choice and bodily autonomy must first be eliminated to achieve it," Mastrine said in a statement.

In an online editorial for *Playboy*, Lucy Steigerwald, a contributing editor to Antiwar.com, acknowledged that excluding women from draft registration was "unfair" and "sexist."

"But the solution to the decrepit notion that the young of the country are communal property is not to remove the sexism, it's to remove the draft," she wrote.

Like Mastrine, Steigerwald supports equal access to the military for women, but opposes conscription. She does not believe, as some have argued, that the return of the draft would make the U.S. more cautious about engaging in conflicts.

"You don't stop the runaway truck of U.S. foreign policy by throwing a man in front of it, and you definitely don't stop it by throwing a man and a woman, just to make things equal," Steigerwald wrote.

The linking of women's equality to universal conscription dates back to the early 1980s. Draft registration had ended in 1975 with the conclusion of the Vietnam War. In 1980, a nervous President Jimmy Carter, alarmed over the Soviet Union's invasion of Afghanistan, reinstated registration to demonstrate U.S. war readiness. Carter actually wanted universal draft registration, but Congress limited the mandate to men.

The male-only system was quickly challenged as sex discrimination. In 1981, a group of men brought a case before the Supreme Court that argued being singled out for compulsory registration violated their right to equal protection. A number of women's groups, including the National Organization for Women (NOW), filed briefs contending that exclusion from the draft violated the constitutional rights of women.

"Compulsory universal military service is central to the concept of citizenship in a democracy," the NOW brief asserted. It predicted "devastating long-term psychological and political repercussions" would result if women were excluded from "the compulsory involvement in the community's survival that is perceived as entitling people to lead it and to derive from it the full rights and privileges of citizenship."

A similar brief filed by 12 other women's organizations, including the League of Women Voters, argued that exempting women from draft registration echoed "the stereotypic notions about women's proper place in society that in the past promoted 'protective' labor laws and the exclusion of women from juries."

NOW had previously opposed the draft, and its apparent about-face infuriated its members at the grassroots level, according to Cynthia Enloe, a research professor of political science and women's studies at Clark University in Worcester, Mass.

Enloe, who has written extensively on women and the military, said she was just starting her research at the time, but as she recalls, "The local chapters were really angry. They were full of women activists who disagreed, who saw the draft as something to oppose."

So why the switch? Enloe thinks it had more to do with NOW's then-recent defeat in getting the Equal Rights Amendment passed than it did zeal for military service. The amendment, which pacifist Alice Paul originally penned in 1923, simply states, "Equality under the law shall not be denied or abridged by the United States or by any State on account of sex." After Congress passed it in 1972, NOW led the unsuccessful fight for its ratification at the state level during the 1970s and early 1980s.

Eleanor Smeal, at the time president of NOW, "had just gone through a terrible defeat," Enloe noted. "When the next thing comes up, you tend to see it through the lens of what you were defeated by. The people in the Washington office were terribly affected by the anti-ERA battle."

Speaking in defense of the NOW brief back in 1981, Smeal told *The New York Times* that wherever she lobbied for the Equal Rights Amendment, male legislators frequently said to her, "When you women fight in a war, then we'll talk about equal rights."

That "argument of entitlement," Smeal said, helped persuade her that exclusion from the draft hurt the interests of women. Ever since ancient Egypt, "the secondary class has not been given the right to serve in the military," she told the newspaper.

Lory Manning, a retired U.S. Navy captain, echoes that thought today, noting, "Except for taxes, women have had to fight for the right to the assumption of the duties of citizenship, including jury duty"

A senior researcher at Service Women's Action Network (SWAN), Manning said she remembers well the antiwar feminism of the Vietnam War era, and agrees with its critique of the military.

"It is hierarchical," she said, "It is also very powerful. People think that an organization with that kind of power should not be left to men. Having women on the ground as peacekeepers has shown to improve the fate of women on the other side."

Like many feminists, Enloe thinks it is risky to frame any military issue around just equality. "A lot of feminists were not sure how to articulate their support for gays in the military," she said. "Those against the ban found themselves having to promote gay men and lesbians as the perfect soldier."

It's a dilemma Enloe said her European counterparts do not face.

"While there are many societies which are more militarized than the U.S., militarism has sunk its roots down so deep in U.S. popular culture, it's made a conundrum of how you carve out a space of equality without embracing military ideals of citizenship," she said.

"The acuteness of this political, cultural dilemma is much sharper in the U.S. than in Europe," she said. "European feminists have been surprised at the prevalence of the military's footprint in our civilian settings. Most soccer games in Europe don't start with fighter jet flyovers."

In 1981, the U.S. Supreme Court upheld a male-only system for draft registration, arguing that since women were "excluded from combat service" they were not "similarly situated" as men for the draft or draft registration. In this instance, the court said, Congress had the authority to consider "military need" over "equity."

With the removal of combat restrictions for women last December, that argument no longer applies. Maria Santelli, at the Washington, D.C.-based Center on Conscience and War, said it is quite likely the courts could soon strike down the current male-only system of draft registration on grounds of discrimination. "Before Congress lets that happen, they might vote for universal conscription," she said.

Santelli thinks improvement in equity and justice within the military is a good thing, but these improvements are overridden by the "other justice issue, which is our reliance on war as a means for conflict resolution," she said.

She pointed out that men who oppose draft registration for reasons of conscience face numerous penalties. Under what is commonly known as "the Solomon Amendment," these penalties include denial of federal student loans, federal job training, and employment with federal executive agencies, and denial of citizenship to immigrants. According to the Center on Conscience and

War, there are Solomon-like penalties in 44 states, with some denying state employment, state student loans, a driver's license, or photo ID to nonregistrants.

"These laws penalize men for the rest of their lives," Santelli said. "Do we want to put women in that same position?"

1. In response to extending the draft to women, some argue that equality with men is meaningless if it robs women of autonomy. Do you think universal conscription should exist for men and women?

2. Some feminists argue that having women "on the ground" is good for both sides of a conflict. Do you agree that women can steer the military in a more ethical direction?

"THE ELECTION INSPIRED THESE 9 WOMEN TO FIGHT BACK AGAINST MISOGYNY IN THEIR OWN LIVES," BY ANNA SILMAN, FROM *NEW YORK MAGAZINE* OCTOBER 18, 2016

As gender issues have increasingly become central to this election – from Trump's taped "locker-room talk" to the wave of sexual-harassment allegations that followed – it's been easy to start feeling hopeless. The excitement of a woman approaching the White House is tempered by the vile misogyny of her opponent, who will eagerly gaslight, humiliate, and exploit women in order to stop her getting there.

But there's something of a silver lining to the nastiness. Trump's egregious behavior — in addition to laying bare GOP misogyny — is making it impossible to ignore the ongoing realities of sexism in this country. And many women are seizing this moment to make their voices heard. As the presidential campaign enters its final throes, I spoke to nine women about how this election has moved them to fight back against misogyny in their own lives, and how they plan to carry that mission forward beyond November 8.

PIPER, 24, DIGITAL ARCHIVIST

"Not only is this my first time voting for a Democrat, but up until a few months ago, I was a red-blooded, rural, Christian conservative from North Dakota. For the first time, hearing the sexism, hatred, and fear in Trump's message opened my eyes to the insidious ways that I had been allowing sexism and the patriarchy to govern my life, but had always made excuses for it, justified it, and managed to ignore it because it was in less-offensive packaging. While his words are like barbed wire, the message is the same when coming out of the bills and legislation from more reasonable party members. Now I can't look away. Thanks to Trump, I'm a newly awoken woman and am proselytizing everyone in my family, my hometown, my (former) church, everyone from my old life: It's easy to denounce a dog who's barking this loudly, but whether he's howling or not barking at all, he (and the party at large) are the same dog.

Everyone else in my life, though, has really engaged in the conversation and, for the first time, we're willing to discuss the 'sacred' GOP in a critical light. My formerly conservative boyfriend has come with me on this journey and now freely admits to being a feminist himself, though a few months ago, before this election cycle, I think through perpetuated misinformation, he would have considered it a dirty or shameful word."

LANI, 45, PROFESSOR

"My female colleagues and I have an informal network to help us navigate the sexual predators or rampant misogynists in our midst. We will warn each other about the bad behavior in various departments so we can navigate ourselves and our students away from those places. It seems like the typical strategy of the powerless, doesn't it?

I recently I got an email from somebody in one of these known departments. The email had a job and asked me to send potential candidates their way. Instead of ignoring it or deleting it like I might normally do, I decided to write back. I let the sender know that their department was known for having an unchecked sexual predator in their midst. I let the sender know that under no circumstances would I advise a junior colleague to take a position in the department given the nonresponse of the administration to complaints that I know were lodged by some of my colleagues there.

I am quite clear that this shift in my response comes out of my frustration at how women are continually silenced and how this response, in turn, manages to protect toxic bad behavior. But I also know that we often feel powerless because our complaints are met with nonresponses by universities. I hope that withholding potential strong candidates can incentivize universities to do better. I think, like many women, I am fed up with our silence around chronic abusers. It was right after Sunday's debate that I chose to respond in that way. The connection was quite clear."

ASHLEY, 35, PUBLIC-RELATIONS PROFESSIONAL

"In my high-school years I was a pretty active member of the local riot-grrrl scene, but as I got older I sort of fell out of touch with my own feminism until this election. It's brought me closer to the women in my life - my mom, my sister, and my friends of all forms of feminism — people of color, LGBT women, and my concerns lie in how we keep this going past November 8. Just because misogyny right now has a face and a name in Donald Trump, doesn't mean it is done.

One of the ways I'm thinking about extending this beyond November is by becoming more engaged in political issues impacting women on a local and state level, especially looking at things like equal pay, health care, and parental leave. I'm also taking a more active role in my profession to mentor and support younger women to develop more confidence in sharing ideas and owning their seat at the table. I think the biggest change in behavior is looking at women's issues beyond those that directly impact me. Being less selfish with my feminism and thinking about how political policy impacts women of all ages around the world. I feel closer to the women around me as we've shared our experiences with misogyny and learned a lot from some of their particular experiences as women of color and LGBT women. My mom and I haven't always seen eye-to-eye on who we vote for, but as a nurse she's felt a lot of sexism in the workplace, and that's drawn us closer together."

SONIA, 30, WRITER

"After the [*Access Hollywood*] video came out, what I saw happening on Twitter was the cycle of making jokes about this phrase. But I was like: I actually think that's very much a real thing, and not everyone realized that. And women who had experienced that maybe felt like they were floundering, because it's really confusing when something that has happened to you, that made you feel like a victim and was traumatizing, hits the news cycle, because then you are facing it regularly. And then, when it becomes something that is funny, it minimizes what it really is.

So I posted this thing on my Twitter that was like: I'm sure that a lot of women are remembering the time this happened to them, and if this has happened to you, share it. It seemed important to share what that story was. So I started doing that, and I was surprised at how many responses I got. It was pretty crazy how many women responded from all kinds of ages, like, *I was walking on the street, or in a boardroom, or in a concert.* It was really intense – responses kept coming in. So many women were saying: This is this thing that sounds like a joke, and this is the reality that we live in. And I wasn't quite prepared for the reality that we live in, that so many women could say something that was so upsetting. It was both me trying to make a point and me realizing a point. It was pretty emotional hearing all of this. It sort of has felt like this is the only thing I can do.

What's cool is I've seen women with much bigger follower counts do the same thing. It sort of seems like there's this massive catharsis happening where a lot of women who wouldn't have felt comfortable to speak up even a couple of years ago are realizing that they don't have to be afraid of what will happen, and maybe that this entire convulsive moment of horribleness is also an opportunity to talk about it, as painful as it is."

JEN*, 26, FREELANCE PRODUCER

"I think even in my adulthood, even until very recently, and kind of even now, I have this weird thing in my head of, *Oh, sex is a compromise.* Which it can be. But I think I have never really stood firm in my ability to say no to things. We have this idea that women have the right to say no, but I've always thought of that as, 'I have the right to say no to a stranger.' I never really thought about that as, 'Oh, I have the right to say no to someone I like and care about, because I still have autonomy.' And I think my view is kind of shifting about what I'm willing to take or not take.

I had some very interesting conversations when the Donald Trump stuff came out, partially because I tweeted a story about experiencing a sexual assault. Guys started tweeting at me saying, *Oh my god, this is so terrible, I can't believe women go through this, what can we do to help?* And then I thought through the guys in my life who generally think of themselves as respectful towards women, and who I generally think of as respectful towards women, but when I got into bed with them it was like: *No, you pushed me way too far, over and over again.* I think one of the things we can do is help the 'good guys' to see their blind spots. So, I called some of those guys who had made me uncomfortable and actually had some amazing conversations. Because there are things like that that I remember so unbelievably vividly, because I was so uncomfortable at the time, that they hardly remember at all.

There was one situation that made me immensely uncomfortable. So I wanted to talk to the guy about it. I tried to talk to him about it that morning, but he wouldn't hear it, and then when I eventually did bring it up, he kept shutting me down. And that night rang in my head over and over because it was so uncomfortable for me. So we hadn't talked in a while and I emailed him, and I was just like, *Hey, it's been a while, but do you think we could have a conversation?* And I don't know if it's because time went by or what, but we talked, and we had the conversation, and I tried to tell him in very calm terms, like, *I'm not here to attack you, I just need you to know this is how I felt, and I just want you to be aware of it for the future.* And he was amazingly responsive. Of course, one conversation doesn't solve anything, but I'm kind of happy that he kind of gets it."

EMILY, 28, JOURNALIST

"In general, I've noticed that I've really been relishing the moments when I'm surrounded exclusively by women. I've also realized how lucky I am to have those moments automatically as a part of my day since I work on an all-female team in the fashion industry. I feel like that's a luxury and a built-in support group not many women get to experience in their lives.

This past Friday, I was egged by a man while having a conversation with friends in a courtyard about creating safe spaces for women – After our initial shock, the experience weirdly bonded us together and allowed us to have a deeper conversation and open up about previous experiences of violence or alienation we've had in our lives."

COLLEEN, PHD STUDENT AND RESEARCHER

"While a graduate student at Duke, I was sexually assaulted. Due to a combination of denial, exhaustion, and fear of professional judgment, I didn't follow up on my police report. I later found out that this man had sexually assaulted other graduate students in the area and had a history of sexual solicitation and abuse of children. Knowing this, I decided I could no longer stay silent, and I agreed to provide testimony in child-custody and physical-assault charges against him at the time. He then threatened me and told me that his partner was a prominent staff member at Duke, and that they had accessed my records, that they knew things about me, and that they would make me be silent.

This election cycle has shown me that no matter how high-achieving, every woman is susceptible to sexual harassment and violence. This has inspired me to share my own stories of assault and harassment more broadly, because it is important that more women and men know that sexual assault doesn't happen to just one type of woman and that victims shouldn't be embarrassed because of what they have been through. [Becoming involved in grad-student unionization efforts on campus] is for me an effort to ensure that there are external bodies which monitor and prevent what happened to me from ever happening to another women or child, and in so doing, return the university to its place as a source of light, knowledge, and right in society."

AINSLEY, 28, SOFTWARE DESIGNER

"Watching the unbelievable double standards of this election, I've been motivated to redraw the division of domestic labor in my own relationship and talk my female friends through the same.

I feel like there has been a noticeable shift in the women that I talk to everyday in my life. What I noticed happening is, overall, there has been general lower tolerance for this kind of stuff, whether it's situations in the workplace, or out in public on the street, or the sort of normalized things that play out in our hetero relationships. I was having these conversations with some of my women friends in a Slack group, sharing complaints, those of us who live with our boyfriends, about how much we do, and how it's so difficult to get them to meet us halfway. I realized I had to lay out all the things that I did without asking or that were going unnoticed. There were so many things I took on by default.

Watching the election play out and seeing how much work women have to do to be considered the equal of men made me angry, and I started reading more about feminism and realizing that the progress that we've made hasn't gotten us out of traditionally female responsibilities. So, like when women went back to work, it didn't mean we weren't still expected to keep our places looking clean. These dynamics are still playing out."

VINCA, 26, GRAD STUDENT

"I'm planning to volunteer on Election Day. I have volunteered before, in 2008, working on the Obama campaign a little bit. I phone banked and handed out ballots. But Trump is so scary. And as a woman, I don't know if I would feel safe in a country run by him, and I don't know if my friends, who are other things that are not white men, would feel safe in a country run by him. I live in Toronto, and I'm only [back home in Chicago] for six days, and I was not planning on using one of them volunteering – but yeah. He's just so scary."

Name has been changed.

1. Do you think these personal narratives of political consciousness represent a "silver lining" to the divisive and ugly 2016 election?

2. Many of the above testimonials deal with aspects of rape culture. Do you think the 2016 election helped women confront this reality?

CHAPTER 3

WHAT THE COURTS SAY

The Supreme Court of the United States (SCOTUS) has periodically acted as an ally to women in their fight for political and civil rights, equal pay, and bodily autonomy. Beginning in 1919, the court ratified the Nineteenth Amendment, giving women the right to vote. Protection against discrimination based on sex was secured in the Civil Rights Act of 1964. As Sarah Azaransky explains in her profile of legal scholar Pauli Murray, the word "sex" in Title VII of the Civil Rights Act was nearly omitted. Some believed that it would distract from the law's impact on racial discrimination. However, Murray believed that racial discrimination was inseparable from gender discrimination, with both "only different phases of the fundamental and indivisible issue of human rights." For this reason, Azaransky credits Murray as being a forerunner to contemporary modes of intersectional thinking.

Another landmark case that proved to be beneficial for women was, of course, *Roe v. Wade* in 1971. The *Roe* ruling legalized a woman's right to an abortion within twenty weeks of conception. The decision gave states latitude in determining the specifics of later-term abortions. In recent years, many states have imposed tougher and tougher abortion restrictions. Has this been an over-reach? Based on the Supreme Court's opinion on Texas law HB 2, it appears many of these restrictive efforts by states will be deemed unconstitutional.

In the high court, progress on feminist issues has perhaps been painfully slow, but by most indicators we are still moving forward incrementally. One thing is clear: Our next president's judicial appointments will be crucial in keeping this momentum and not turning back the clock on women's basic rights. In the final selection of this chapter, Michele L. Swers articulates these concerns regarding what Donald Trump's presidency could mean for women.

"US SUPREME COURT STOPS THE SHAM BY STRIKING DOWN TEXAS ABORTION LAW," BY DIERDRE FULTON, FROM *COMMON DREAMS*, JUNE 27, 2016

Women's health advocates rejoiced on Monday as the U.S. Supreme Court overturned Texas' controversial abortion restrictions, saying they pose an unconstitutional burden.

Justice Anthony Kennedy sided with four liberal justices for a 5-3 decision (pdf) in *Whole Woman's Health v. Hellerstedt*, considered the biggest abortion case since *Roe v. Wade*.

"I am beyond elated," said lead plaintiff Amy Hagstrom Miller, founder and CEO of the Whole Woman's Health network of providers. "Every day Whole Woman's Health treats our patients with compassion, respect and dignity—and with this historic decision, today the Supreme Court did the same. We're thrilled that justice was served and our clinics stay open."

She continued: "After years of fighting heartless, anti-abortion Texas politicians who would seemingly stop at nothing to push abortion out of reach, I want everyone to understand: you don't mess with Texas, you don't mess with Whole Woman's Health, and you don't mess with this beautiful, powerful movement of people dedicated to reproductive health, rights, and justice."

The case concerned two provisions of a 2013 law known as HB2, one requiring all abortion providers to obtain local hospital admitting privileges and another mandating that every reproductive health care facility offering abortion services to meet the same hospital-like building standards as an ambulatory surgical center. Reproductive health advocates said the law would have forced all but a handful of abortion clinics in the state to close—and its burdensome requirements were already hindering access across the state.

Vicki Saporta, president and CEO of the National Abortion Federation (NAF), said that since the passage of HB2, her organization's hotline has been "flooded with calls from Texas women desperately trying to access the abortion care they need."

"Too many of those women," she said, "after hearing how far they would have to travel to access care, simply said 'I can't get there.' Other women have made appointments, hopeful they could find someone to drive them, only to have to cancel at the last minute. We've even heard from women forced to spend the night in their car because they couldn't afford a hotel or another round-trip to the clinic. Hopefully, with this decision, new high-quality clinics will be able to open in Texas and throughout the U.S. and women will be able to access abortion care closer to home."

Under the banner "Stop the Sham," the plaintiffs had said all along that the HB2 restrictions were in fact aimed not at protecting women's health—as their anti-choice proponents claimed—but at closing down clinics.

In their ruling, the justices appeared to concur. "We conclude that neither of these provisions offers medical benefits sufficient to justify the burdens upon access that each imposes," Justice Stephen Breyer wrote for the majority.

On the admitting privileges requirement, the court found "there was no significant health-related problem that the new law helped to cure."

The opinion continues:

We have found nothing in Texas' record evidence that shows that, compared to prior law (which required a "working arrangement" with a doctor with admitting, the new law advanced Texas' legitimate interest in protecting women's health.

We add that, when directly asked at oral argument whether Texas knew of a single instance in which the new requirement would have helped even one woman obtain better treatment, Texas admitted that there was no evidence in the record of such a case.

Meanwhile, the justices point to medical evidence showing the surgical-center requirement "is not necessary" and would likely result in overcrowded facilities serving five times their usual number of patients:

More fundamentally, in the face of no threat to women's health, Texas seeks to force women to travel long distances to get abortions in crammed-to-capacity superfacilities. Patients seeking these services are less likely to get the kind of individualized attention, serious conversation, and emotional support that doctors at less taxed facilities may have offered. Healthcare facilities and medical professionals are not fungible commodities. Surgical centers attempting to accommodate sudden, vastly increased demand...may find that quality of care declines.

"Today, women across the nation have had their constitutional rights vindicated," declared Nancy Northup, president and CEO of the Center for Reproductive Rights. "The Supreme Court sent a loud and clear message that politicians cannot use deceptive means to shut down abortion clinics."

But even as they celebrated, reproductive rights experts warned that the struggle continues.

"The fight to protect abortion access does not end today—this is just the first step in dismantling laws that make it harder for people to access the health care they need," said Heather Busby, executive director of NARAL Pro-Choice Texas.

Indeed, American College of Obstetricians and Gynecologists president Thomas Gellhaus wrote at *Rewire* ahead of Monday's ruling, "even if we are able to celebrate a favorable outcome in the case, the battle for reproductive health will continue in dozens of states across the country."

Similar Targeted Regulation of Abortion Providers, or TRAP, laws have been passed around the country, he said, "and in some cases, their implementation will depend on the outcome of *Whole Woman's Health.*"

The ACLU, which said the effects of the decision will likely be felt around the country, noted that challenges to admitting privileges requirements similar to the Texas law are currently pending in federal courts in Alabama, Louisiana, Mississippi, Tennessee, and Wisconsin.

1. The banner "stop the sham" indicates the surreptitious manner in which lawmakers tried to limit women's access to abortion. Now that so-called TRAP laws such as HB 2 have been deemed unconstitutional, do you think abortion opponents will continue with or abandon this tactic?

> 2. Do you think similar laws restricting abortion in other states will be overturned or upheld?

"JANE CROW: PAULI MURRAY'S INTERSECTIONS AND ANTIDISCRIMINATION LAW," BY SARAH AZARANSKY, FROM THE *JOURNAL OF FEMINIST STUDIES* IN RELIGION, SPRING 2013

In this article, I discuss Pauli Murray's significant contributions to American jurisprudence, including her conceptualization of the category of Jane Crow and her efforts to have "sex" added to Title VII of the 1964 Civil Rights Act. By considering Jane Crow as a precursor to Kimberle Crenshaw's theory of intersectionality, I argue that Murray's work provides contemporary scholars and democratic activists with resources for thinking about legal subjects as embodied persons at intersections of sexual, gender, and racial identities. While the focus here is on Murray's legal career, I underscore how Murray characterized legal questions as moral and spiritual problems, thus inviting scholars and activists from other disciplines to develop moral and legal analysis that may help the law respond to embodied realities.

Pauli Murray's illustrious legal career began in the early 1940s while she was a student at Howard Law School. Though leading civil rights scholars trained her to confront Jim Crow, Murray left Howard with a keen sense of what she called Jane Crow. After her male classmates and professors repeatedly diminished women's concerns, Murray recognized that she was, "a minority within a minority, with all the built-in disadvantages that such status entailed."[1] In a 1947 article, she described Jane Crow as African American women's experiences of being discriminated against as a result of racism *and* sexism. Murray distinguished Jane Crow from white women's and black men's concerns, "for within this framework of 'male supremacy' as well as 'white supremacy,' the Negro woman finds herself at the bottom of the economic and social scale."[2] Murray would use Jane Crow in her legal and religious writing to explain how African American women experience an interstructuring of oppressions.

SEX AND ANTIDISCRIMINATION LAW: A NEW LEGAL STRATEGY

In her early career, Pauli Murray distinguished herself as an employment and antidiscrimination law expert, who insisted on the indivisibility of human rights.[3] She was among a group of feminist lawyers developing legal strategies to move forward women's rights. Amid debates about landmark civil rights legislation, this group seized the chance to expand legal protections for women. The word "sex" was a last minute amendment to Title VII, which prohibits workplace discrimination, of the House's version of the Civil Rights Act and was expected to be removed by the Senate. The initial wording precluded employment discrimination "according to a person's race, color, religion, or national origin"; the proposed amendment added "sex." This group of feminist lawyers tapped

Murray to write a memo in support of retaining "sex" that would be sent to lawmakers and White House officials.

Opponents of the amendment of "sex" believed that it would distract from the Civil Rights Act's primary purpose—to end discrimination against African Americans. But Murray saw this as a false dichotomy: she opened the memo with a comparison between the status of (white) women and (male) African Americans. Drawing such a comparison, or using analogical reasoning, was a familiar strategy in legal writing whereby she could take advantage of recent civil rights precedents by "applying accepted principles to new circumstances."[4] Citing evidence from contemporary social scientists about simi-larities between sex and race discrimination, Murray emphasized that while courts had worked to remedy race discrimination, they were almost completely oblivious to sex discrimination.

In defense of keeping "sex" in Title VII, Murray argued initially that sexism is as destructive as racism. To convince lawmakers about the importance of the amendment, Murray drew a number of parallels between race discrimination (which senators were ready to legis-late against) and sex discrimination (which they largely overlooked). In 1964, Murray was among the first legal theorists to associate sex and race discrimination. In fact, legal scholar Serena Mayeri argues that "no one did more than Murray to make race-sex analogies the legal currency of feminism."[5]

However, Murray's argument did not rest on an equivalency between racism and sexism. Her comparison was rhetorically strategic, leading readers to see the moral significance of sexism. She then insisted that race and sex discrimination should not be separated, for they were "only different phases of the fundamental and indivisible issue of human rights."[6] Rather than merely parallel, Murray affirmed that race and sex discrimination were connected and she invoked the experiences of African American women to demonstrate overlapping and interconnected forms of inequality. Murray cited demographic reports about the synthetic forms of inequality that a black woman endured, for she had less education, earned less, was in the labor market longer, and bore a heavier economic burden of heading a family. Murray concluded that "in a more sharply defined struggle than is apparent in any other social group in the United States, [a black woman] is literally engaged in a battle for sheer survival."[7]

Standing at the intersection of the century's two great social movements, Pauli Murray argued that "these two types of discrimination are so closely intertwined and so similar that [black] women are uniquely qualified to affirm their interrelatedness."[8] Including "sex" in Title VII *would* protect black workers, because, like Murray herself, many black workers were women. Murray's memo was sent to a select group of senators, White House officials, Attorney General Robert F. Kennedy, and Lady Bird Johnson. Murray was convincing: The Senate retained "sex" in Title VII.

Murray's rhetorical shift from comparing race and sex discrimination to reveal African American women's synthetic experiences of racism and sexism illuminated a blind spot in legal theorizing about discrimination. In arguing on behalf of retaining "sex" in Title VII, Murray did not simply rest on analogical reasoning, rather she pushed toward a new horizon in legal analysis that recognized how women who were black experienced racism and how blacks who were women experienced sexism. By focusing on African American women, Murray explained that for antidiscrimination law to work, it must take into account how different types of discrimination may overlap and reinforce each other.

In her arguments about Title VII, Murray anticipated ongoing efforts in critical race feminism for the law to be responsive to actual identities—to bodies that are female and black, for example. In 1989, Kimberle Crenshaw developed the category of intersectionality to describe discrimination that occurs at the intersection of race and sex (as well as class, on the basis of sexuality, and so on). With "black women as [her] starting point," Crenshaw described how "intersectional experience is greater than the sum of racism and sexism."[9] She reviewed a series of well-known rulings in which black women used Title VII to make intersectional claims—when plaintiffs appealed to more than one aspect of identity—and found that courts rejected black women's multiple claims. Emblematic of the courts' inability to conceive the intersectional nature of identity was the ruling in *DeGraffenreid v. General Motors*, a 1977 case in which five African American women claimed that they were adversely affected because of their race and sex by a "last hired-first fired" policy.

In rejecting the women's claims, the judge wrote, "the plaintiffs are clearly entitled to a remedy if they have been discriminated against. However, they should not be allowed to combine statutory remedies to create a new 'super-remedy' which would give them relief beyond what the drafters of the relevant statutes intended."[10] That is, plaintiffs weren't allowed to claim race *and* sex discrimination. Crenshaw pointed out how rulings like this ignore how identity actually works. In her writing, it's not clear whether Crenshaw knew of Murray's contributions (Crenshaw does not cite Murray). But Murray's readers know that she didn't just understand how intersectionality operates. Perhaps more important, as someone who worked to shape the relevant statute, she also did in fact intend for Title VII to be used to make intersectional claims. Yet almost forty years after Murray's work, to have the law be responsive to the intersection of race and sex, antidiscrimination law has not protected people who make so-called multiple claims.

In the past few years, legal theorists have undertaken empirical studies of Crenshaw's 1989 hypothesis that intersectional plaintiffs fare worse in discrimination lawsuits. In a 2009 article, Minna Kotkin argued that "empirical evidence demonstrates that multiple claims are all but impossible to win," but, at the same time, that multiple claims are growing rapidly.[11] Kotkin noted that since the era of *DeGraffenreid*, intersectional claims under Title VII have increased significantly. In the 1970s and 1980s, for example, about 10 percent of plaintiffs made intersectional claims; by the 1990s, that percentage had climbed to 25 percent. But the odds of attaining either a partial or complete victory are slim.[12] In a 2011 article, Rachel Best and her coauthors reported that their own empirical study of intersectionality cases found that "anti-discrimination lawsuits provide the least protection for those who already suffer multiple social disadvantages."[13]

LEGACIES OF MURRAY'S WORK

Now back to Murray: other than offering an interesting historical footnote to work on intersectionality—that someone who worked to shape Title VII did indeed have a theory of intersectional identity—what can Murray offer us that we can make use of today? I think many things, but I will conclude by pointing to two legacies of Murray's work that can contribute to contemporary work in a common freedom struggle, by which I mean a movement for political and economic change that includes identifying and addressing long-term, systemic discrimination.[14]

The first legacy is the importance of moral imagination to legal theory and argument. In an oral interview Murray gave before ordination she said that she felt called because, "the particular profession to which I had devoted the larger section of my life, law, was—that we had reached a point where law could not give us the answers."[15] Murray's move away from the law to explore her religious vocation ought not to be read as a wholesale rejection of the law as useful for human rights advocacy. Since the majority of the aforementioned interview is devoted to Murray's legal work, it is judicious to interpret Murray's professional shift as a result, in part, of the law not giving us *all* the answers.

Indeed, Murray affirmed that her legal work convinced her that "all the problems of human rights, ... were [basically] moral and spiritual problems."[16] What did she mean by this? Throughout her legal writing--and her vast trove of political essays, her family memoir, and into her sermons—Murray repeatedly used herself and her family's history as paradigmatic of American identity. In other words, Murray situated herself, an African American woman, as a primary democratic subject, rather than as a problem or an exception. And so, while Murray shifted her professional attention from law to ministry, we can hear her in the challenge that Crenshaw laid out and on which others have reflected: How can we develop a theory of antidiscrimination law that responds to actual bodies, while not treating those bodies as a problem or exception? This is also a question for feminist scholars in religion. We should be in conversation with people at law schools to recover voices like Murray's, who urge us to develop modes of moral and legal analysis that will lead to making intersectional claims more viable.

The second legacy is the lesson that we must develop multiracial coalitions. Murray always argued that, as an African American woman, her own interests could only be represented by a coalition, that narrow, univocal, or single-axis organizing around a discrete identity could only partially represent her. She saw what Cornel West argues today: that for us to transform the country from a racist to a nonracist one, we must learn to organize in multiracial coalitions.[17] Coalitions, argues West today and argued Murray in the last century, are crucial to Left politics, because the Left isn't strong enough to transform society without them. Murray's moral imagination can broaden our own: it encourages us to identify and address long-term, systemic discrimination and to build effective coalitions in order that more justice is available for more people.

1. Most of the work on intersectionality we have encountered is focused on identity politics. Do Murray and Crenshaw's early intersectionality theories differ meaningfully in approach? If so, how?

2. Later in her career, Pauli Murray turned away from the law, claiming all problems of human rights were essentially moral and spiritual issues. Do you agree?

"WHY WE NEED THE EQUAL RIGHTS AMENDMENT," FROM THE *ALICE PAUL INSTITUTE* (API)

- Section 1. Equality of rights under the law shall not be denied or abridged by the United States or by any state on account of sex.
- Section 2. The Congress shall have the power to enforce, by appropriate legislation, the provisions of this article.
- Section 3. This amendment shall take effect two years after the date of ratification.

- Without the ERA, the Constitution does not explicitly guarantee that the rights it protects are held equally by all citizens without regard to sex. The first — and still the only — right specifically affirmed as equal for women and men is the right to vote.
- The equal protection clause of the Constitution's 14th Amendment was first applied to sex discrimination only in 1971, and it has never been interpreted to grant equal rights on the basis of sex in the uniform and inclusive way that the ERA would.

- The ERA would provide a clearer judicial standard for deciding cases of sex discrimination, since federal and state courts (some working with state ERAs, some without) still reflect confusion and inconsistency in dealing with such claims. It would also clarify sex discrimination jurisprudence and conclusively invalidate the claim of the late Supreme Court Justice Antonin Scalia that the Constitution, specifically the 14th Amendment, does not protect against sex discrimination (reported in *California Lawyer*, January 2011).
- The ERA would provide a strong legal defense against a rollback of the significant advances in women's rights that have been achieved since the mid–20th century.
- Without the ERA, women regularly and men occasionally have to fight long, expensive, and difficult legal battles in an effort to prove that their rights are equal to those of the other sex.
- The ERA would improve the United States' standing in the world community with respect to human rights. The governing documents of many other countries affirm legal gender equality, however imperfect the global implementation of that ideal may be.

After more than a generation of significant advances for women, do we still need the Equal Rights Amendment? The answer is an unqualified yes! Legal sex discrimination is not yet a thing of the past, and the progress of the past 60 years is not irreversible. Some remaining inequities result more from individual behavior and social practices than from legal discrimination, but they can all be influenced by a strong message that the Constitution has zero tolerance for any form of sex discrimination. Thus, the reasons why we need the ERA are at one level philosophical and symbolic, and at another level very specific and practical.

The Equal Rights Amendment is needed to affirm constitutionally that the bedrock principles of our democracy — "all men are created equal," "liberty and justice for all," "equal justice under law," "government of the people, by the people, and for the people" — apply equally to women.

In principle:

It is necessary to have specific language in the Constitution affirming the principle of equal rights on the basis of sex because for more than two centuries, women have had to fight long and hard political battles to win rights that men (at first certain white men, eventually all men) possessed automatically because they were male. The first — and still the only — right that the Constitution specifically affirms equally for women and men is the right to vote. Alice Paul introduced the ERA in 1923 to expand that affirmation to all the rights guaranteed by the Constitution.

It was not until as recently as 1971 that the 14th Amendment's equal protection clause was first applied to sex discrimination. Even today, a major distinction between the sexes is present from the moment of birth — the different legal standing of males and females with respect to how their constitutional rights are obtained. As demonstrated in 1996 by the last major Supreme Court decision on sex discrimination, which dealt with admission of women to Virginia Military Institute (VMI), we have not moved beyond the traditional assumption that males hold rights and females, if treated unequally, must prove that they hold them. The Equal Rights Amendment would remove that differential assumption.

In practice:

The practical effect of this amendment would be seen most clearly in court deliberations on cases of sex discrimination. For the first time, "sex" would be a suspect classification requiring the same high level of "strict scrutiny" and having to meet the same high level of justification — a "necessary" relation to a "compelling" state interest — that the classification of race currently requires.

The VMI decision now tells courts to exercise "skeptical scrutiny" requiring "exceedingly persuasive" justification of differential treatment on the basis of sex, but prohibition of sex discrimination is still not as strongly enforceable as prohibition of race discrimination. Ironically, under current court decisions about sex and race discrimination, a white male claiming race discrimination by a program or action is protected by strict scrutiny, but a black female claiming sex discrimination by the same program or action is protected by only skeptical, not strict, scrutiny.

We need the ERA to clarify the law for the lower courts, whose decisions still reflect confusion and inconsistency about how to deal with sex discrimination claims. If the ERA were in the Constitution, it would in many cases influence the tone of legal reasoning and decisions regarding women's equal rights, producing over time a cumulative positive effect.

The Equal Rights Amendment is needed in order to prevent a rollback of women's rights by conservative/reactionary political votes, and to promote laws and court decisions that fairly take into account women's as well as men's experiences.

In principle:

Aren't there already enough legal prohibitions of sex discrimination — the Equal Pay Act, Title VII and Title IX of the 1964 Civil Rights Act, the Pregnancy Discrimination Act, Supreme Court decisions based on the 14th Amendment's equal protection clause, and more? Why are there still people saying, as Alice Paul did in 1923, "We shall not be safe until the principle of equal rights is written into the framework of our government"?

The need for the ERA can be expressed simply as a warning. Unless we put into the Constitution the bedrock principle that equality of rights cannot be denied or abridged on account of sex, the political and judicial victories women have achieved with their blood, sweat, and tears for over two centuries are vulnerable to erosion or reversal at any time — now or in the future.

Congress has the power to make laws that replace existing laws — and to do so by a simple majority. Therefore, many of the current legal protections against sex discrimination can be removed by the margin of a single vote. While courts in the near term would still apply skeptical scrutiny to laws that differentiate on the basis of sex, that precedent could be undermined or eventually ignored by future conservative or reactionary courts. With a specific constitutional guarantee of equal rights through the Equal Rights Amendment, it would be much harder for legislators and courts to reverse our progress in eliminating sex discrimination.

In practice:

Would anyone really want to turn back the clock on women's advancement? Ask the members of Congress who have tried to cripple Title IX, which requires equal opportunity in education — who have opposed the Violence Against Women Act, the Fair Pensions Act, and the Paycheck Fairness Act — who voted to pay for Viagra for servicemen but oppose funding for family planning and contraception — who for decades have blocked U.S. ratification of the United Nations Convention on the Elimination of All Forms of Discrimination Against Women (CEDAW).

Most laws that discriminated explicitly against women have been removed from the books — in many cases, as a result of the political power and expertise developed by women in the course of the ERA ratification campaign. The current legal and judicial systems, however, still often have an impact on women that works to their disadvantage, because those systems have traditionally used the male experience as the norm.

Therefore, lawmakers and judges must be encouraged to include equitable consideration of female experiences as they deal with issues of Social Security, taxes, wages, pensions, domestic relations, insurance, violence, and more. Without an Equal Rights Amendment providing motivation, the status quo will change much more slowly.

1. Do you support the Equal Rights Amendment, or is this unnecessary given the inclusion of "sex" in Title VII of the Civil Rights Act, and other similar legislation?

2. What are the best arguments for passing the ERA, in your view? Do you think the ERA will ever become part of the Constitution?

"WHAT TRUMP'S ELECTION COULD MEAN FOR WOMEN: FEWER REPRODUCTIVE RIGHTS, NEW HELP FOR WORKING FAMILIES?" BY MICHELE L. SWERS, FROM *THE CONVERSATION*, NOVEMBER 15, 2016

After a bruising campaign that focused heavily on President-elect Trump's treatment of women, what will the new administration mean for women? Overall, Trump paid little attention to women's issues during the campaign. His plans to "make America great again" focused on investing in infrastructure, renegotiating trade agreements, tightening immigration laws and repealing the Affordable Care Act.

But Trump has embraced two policy areas with major implications for women: abortion and help for working families. On reproductive rights he supports traditional Republican policies to restrict the availability of abortion. However, his promises regarding child care and family leave chart new territory for Republican candidates and policymakers. The small contingent of GOP women in Congress could play an important role in shaping Trump's policies on women's issues and selling his proposals to the public.

ROE V. WADE IN THE CROSS-HAIRS

Since Roe v. Wade was decided in 1973, Democrats and Republicans have battled over efforts to restrict abortion rights. In the early 1990s, some members of Congress crossed party lines on this issue. A small contingent of moderate Republicans, many of them women, took pro-choice positions on abortion, while a group of conservative Democrats, generally men, supported pro-life proposals. Today, however, almost all Democrats vote pro-choice, while virtually all Republicans vote pro-life.

Prior to running for president, Trump did not focus on abortion and even espoused pro-choice views. However, as the Republican presidential candidate he staked out pro-life positions, a shift that helped him gain support from social conservatives in the Republican base. Trump pledged to appoint a conservative Supreme Court justices who will overturn Roe v. Wade, and chose Indiana Governor Mike Pence as his running mate. Pence signed numerous abortion restrictions into law as governor and championed proposals to restrict abortion and defund Planned Parenthood while serving in Congress.

The Supreme Court has long been divided on abortion, narrowly upholding Roe v. Wade while allowing states to pass various restrictions on abortion access.

Most recently, in a 5-3 decision issued after Justice Scalia's death, the court overturned a Texas state law that required abortion clinics to meet the standards of surgical facilities and mandated that doctors who work at the clinics have admitting privileges at nearby hospitals. The court ruled that these restrictions would force so many clinics to shut down that women would not have meaningful to access abortion services.

Trump's promise to appoint conservative pro-life jurists has far-reaching implications. Since swing vote Anthony Kennedy and liberal justices Ruth Bader Ginsberg and Steven Breyer are all more than 70 years old, President Trump could reshape the balance of the court on abortion over his four years in office.

More immediately, Trump is likely to support legislative efforts to restrict access to abortion. In 2003, during the last period when Republicans held unified control of Congress and the White House, Congress passed and President George W. Bush signed the first national restriction on an abortion procedure, the Partial-Birth Abortion Act. Overturned by the Supreme Court in 2006, the law was later upheld when President Bush's Supreme Court nominee, Samuel Alito, replaced Sandra Day O'Connor on the court.

Since Republicans won back control of the House in 2010 they have offered several proposals to restrict abortion, including a ban on abortions after 20 weeks' gestation, known as the Pain Capable Unborn Child Protection Act, and numerous efforts to defund Planned Parenthood. The 20-week ban would directly challenge Roe v. Wade because it bans an abortion pre-viability. Under the Roe framework, which was modified by Planned Parenthood v. Casey in 1992 to allow regulations that do not place an "undue burden" on a woman's ability to access abortion, the state cannot put a blanket ban on an abortion procedure before the fetus reaches viability.

As part of efforts to repeal or rewrite the Affordable Care Act, Trump could use executive action to eliminate regulations that require insurance companies to provide women with free access to contraception. House Speaker Paul Ryan has refused to predict whether Congress would retain the ACA's requirement for insurers to cover contraceptives if it overhauls the law.

NEW HELP FOR WORKING FAMILIES?

Trump's stances on child care and family leave could break new ground. With tax reform at the top of House Speaker Ryan's agenda, Trump may be able to push through his proposals to make child care tax deductible, create dependent care savings accounts and incentivize employers to provide child care services. These measures are part of Trump's agenda for his first hundred days in office.

Paid family leave will be a heavier lift in a Republican Congress. Originally conceived by his daughter Ivanka, Trump's proposal would provide six weeks of paid leave to new mothers (but not to fathers), using federal unemployment insurance.

However, Republicans dislike imposing new mandates on business and expanding social welfare programs. In 1990 President George H.W. Bush vetoed the Family and Medical Leave Act, which required employers to provide up to three months of unpaid leave to care for new children or sick family members. Bush's successor, Bill Clinton, immediately signed the FMLA into law upon taking office in 1993.

As an alternative, Republicans have promoted policies that would allow employers to offer employees the option of receiving time off in lieu of overtime pay. The latest version of the bill, sponsored by Alabama Rep. Martha Roby, passed the House in 2013 but was never considered by the Democratic-controlled Senate.

KEY ROLES FOR GOP WOMEN

My research demonstrates that women bring a distinctive perspective to the policymaking table representing the views of various groups of women, including mothers, working women, and women who are caregivers for children and elderly relatives. Trump's daughter Ivanka and campaign manager Kellyanne Conway were able to persuade Trump to consider women's issues during the campaign. So far, however, few women are being considered for top posts in Trump's administration.

There will be only 26 Republican women in the 115th Congress, two fewer than in the 114th Congress, compared to 78 Democratic women. House Republican Conference Chair Cathy McMorris Rodgers of Washington state, the highest-ranking Republican woman in Congress, has worked to reach out to women voters and provide a female perspective in policy deliberations and could be a key Trump ally.

As Republicans move more aggressively to restrict abortion, I expect Democrats will accuse the party of waging a war on women, jeopardizing women's health by taking away access to cancer screenings at Planned Parenthood, contraception and legal safe abortion procedures. Republicans will call on their female members to rebut these attacks.

Support from Republican women in Congress will be crucial for Trump. In 2015, when some GOP women objected to the fact that the proposed 20-week ban did not include a rape exemption, Republican leaders were forced to pull the bill from the floor to accommodate their concerns.

Conversely, abortion rights advocates will count on two key moderate Republicans in the Senate – Maine's Susan Collins and Alaska's Lisa Murkowski – to join Democratic efforts to block abortion legislation through filibusters and negotiations.

If Trump plays to the GOP base and focuses solely on abortion, he will further alienate minority and college-educated women who supported Hillary Clinton. However, if he promotes legislation to make child care more affordable for working families and provide paid leave for new parents, he could gain female supporters – particularly white college-educated women, who voted for Clinton over Trump by a 6-point margin. Increasing his support among these so-called soccer moms, who are traditional Republican voters, will be key to avoiding midterm losses for the party in 2018 and helping Trump position himself for reelection in 2020.

1. Have any of the author's predictions about a Trump presidency come to pass? Which predictions have been most accurate?

2. Supreme Court justices are supposed to evaluate laws impartially. Why might conservative justices be more likely to restrict or repeal *Roe v. Wade*?

CHAPTER 4

WHAT ADVOCACY GROUPS SAY

As with feminist studies in academia, the contemporary landscape of feminist advocacy is marked by differing approaches to understanding and doing feminism. These primarily break down along generational lines. Established groups such as the National Organization for Women (NOW), founded in 1966 by Betty Friedan and Pauli Murray, and the Feminist Majority Foundation, founded in 1987, have a combined membership of nearly one million Americans. These and similar well-funded organizations emerged from the second-wave feminist movement, and focus tirelessly on liberal policy issues such as reproductive rights, equal pay, and anti-discrimination.

Starting around the 1990s, younger voices began infusing feminist advocacy with renewed energy and more nuanced perspectives. These so-called third-wave feminist advocates tend to be less trusting of institutional channels and the mainstream political system, favoring instead to articulate their concerns through micro-politics and other decentralized sites of action. Third-wave feminist advocacy discourses question the primacy of white, middle class women's experience, and are more inclusive of, and responsive to, the need of women of color, the disabled, the LGBT community, and other marginalized groups.

The relative importance of the internet and social media also constitutes a key difference between these approaches to advocacy. Not to suggest that "old-school" feminist advocates cannot operate a computer or use social media effectively, but it would be difficult to imagine establishment feminists getting behind the SlutWalk, chronicled below by Alyssa Teekah. Judging by the backlash this event garnered, it is possible younger feminists can learn from their seniors. Indeed the critique of "hashtag" feminism is that it is ineffectual and exists mostly to serve the psychological needs of its atomized participants.

We will also hear in this chapter from those who reject feminism's liberal predisposition. The conservative Empowered Women group believes "feminism" is a toxic term and wishes to provide "an alternative of fun, engaging accomplished women." Other groups have similarly argued against the label of "feminist" or "feminism," particularly in order to challenge the assumption that only women can be feminists or that feminism affects only women.

"THIS IS WHAT A FEMINIST LOOKS LIKE: FIGHTING RACISM AND SEXISM WITHIN THE FEMINIST MOVEMENT," BY ANGELA MYERS, FROM THE NATIONAL ORGANIZATION FOR WOMEN (NOW), JULY 13, 2016

Wobbly and unsure on her feet, my mom leans with one hand on her walker while the other points to the large pink button on her chest. The button reads, "This is what a feminist looks like." I had given the large button along with a few others with feminist quotes to her for her birthday. By wearing the button, which she dutifully pins to her chest everyday, she breaks stereotypes. Not many people look at disabled Black women and think: "feminism". But she wears her button proudly. I then turn to my father and ask, "Are you a feminist?"

He nods his head and says, "I became a feminist when I had two daughters and realized that gender inequality is a real thing in the workplace,"

I nodded my head, but also knew in my mind that this was untrue. My dad had spent his life researching racial disparities in policy and the prison industrial system. For years he wrote about how Black men's bodies are criminalized, and how it affects families and communities. He would write racism, but in actuality the criminalization of Black men's bodies comes from racism and sexism. From reading his work from the seventies and eighties, I know that he has been a feminist long before he called himself one. For years Critical Race Theorists, Civil Rights activists, and more would not call their work "Feminism" because of the assumed meaning that feminism only fights for women's rights.

And although the majority of feminist activism does fight for women's rights. The true meaning of feminism is to fight against sexism and oppression, which effects everyone. When young boys have sex with their teachers in middle schools, feminist activists call it rape. It was feminist theorists who began to tell boys that accepting kindness and being loving is not emasculating, and that "man up" does not equate to inflicting violence. These are feminist issues. The many men and women who raise these issues are feminists, even if they do not see themselves as such.

When someone says "Feminist," usually the image of a white, privileged, cis-gendered heterosexual woman comes to mind. This stereotype of the typical feminist is becoming increasingly untrue (also historically there were plenty of folk outside this stereotype that held feminist ideals even if they did not call themselves feminists.) Take a quick look at Twitter and the folk who claim Feminism, and you will see that men, transfolk, women of color, presidents, and even my parents claim Feminism.

The stereotype of what a feminist should look like is harmful because it creates an untrue narrative of what feminists fight for. Feminists fight for equality of the sexes. Whatever equality looks like for them. For many People of Color, and others, this also means fighting for racial equality. And by seeing feminists and feminism as a two-dimensional concept that only incorporates a singular view, we disregard the many brilliant and inspirational people who are doing feminist work.

My feminism means fighting for racial justice as well as gender equality. I am a Black woman from Minnesota. On July 7th, 2016, I woke up with my home state in the news. I woke up and saw a Black man, Philando Castille, being shot on a road I've driven on before, with a four year old Black girl and a Black woman also in the car. My first reaction was not surprise. I am no longer surprised when horrific acts of violence are perpetrated by police officers against men of color only to be broadcast to the world. But I am pained. I feel my eyes tear up. I feel my mood darken.

And I remember the last time my state made headlines, it was for being the best state in the country to live in. The truth, which I've known for a while, is that Minnesota is a great state to live in if you are White and Christian. Minnesota has a real race problem. It has one of the highest disproportionate shares of Black folk in prison in the country. This is a sexist problem as well as racist because as we know, Black men aren't inherently more violent or criminal. But still white police officers believe they are. Black children have the highest drowning rates in the country, and are more likely to drown in my state than be shot. Black students in the state are consistently failing in our school systems, many dropping out at some of the highest rates in the country. Islamophobia and xenophobia against the Somali population is obvious. Also many of the women and children who have found refuge in the state suffer from PTSD and often don't get the help they need to thrive, because they are seen as temporary guests. These are never things that are considered in the articles on which state is best.

These facts show that there aren't policies in place in Minnesota that serve the most vulnerable populations. And as legislators don't create policies to protect our communities, they are showing how they don't care about Black communities. Legislators, and also the majority of the White community in Minnesota, are ignorant to the Black communities in Minnesota.

The policies that are in place, put Black bodies in prison. These are sexist policies as well because they rely on stereotypes that are linked to sex and gender. Black skin is not on trial here, but Black bodies are. Being Black in Minnesota is being invisible when it comes to how people make laws and who they are looking at to help, but being hyper-visible in the eyes of law enforcement as a threat, as criminal, as dangerous.

When the word "inclusive" was used in my privileged, predominately white high school, the inclusion was for the LGBTQIA community, not for the students of color. Often issues revolving around LGBT rights and feminism were only linked to white skin and the obstacles that White women faced or White Queer folk faced. And these conversations are important. But the conversations never got far enough to think about Women of Color or Queer People of Color. Our pain and our complexities are invisible in Minnesota. The most common phrase that I heard growing up was that we were the dirt, the shit, the dark hole in the never ending land of snow. If you can imagine that image, you will understand the isolation and the hyper-visibility of what it is like to be Black in Minnesota.

I remember when a cop car slowed to a stop when I was walking down a cold Minneapolis street. My heart raced and although I was doing nothing wrong, all the laws I could be expected to break were on my mind. My throat was dry and I could feel myself holding back tears while I answered the policeman's questions. "How old are you?" "What are you doing out on this street at this time of night?" It was ten and I was walking from my boyfriend's house to where I had parked my car. "Oh where does your *boyfriend* live?" It was then, with the disgust rolling off his body that I knew what he saw. He didn't see an ambitious, high- achieving, varsity swimmer, sixteen-year-old girl in her first relationship. But rather someone more sinister, who didn't deserve to walk the streets of Minneapolis. If I told you what I was wearing, would you believe my innocence? Long johns, jeans, ugg boots, and a large puffy jacket couldn't disway his suspicion. Plenty of people passed me. All of them White. All of them stare, but none of them made eye-contact.

This is what it is like when the intersection of racism and sexism play on your skin. And thinking back I wonder, why couldn't that police officer see a feminist? This would happen more and more as I got older, as my body changed. And as I got older I realized more and more, why I needed feminism, and why fighting just racism or just sexism was not enough. Because when I walk into a room, people do not see just a Black person, or just a woman; they see a Black woman. And because of this, there has never been a time or case when I just felt like a Black person, or just a woman. I do not know what those two things are separately. But feminism fights for me, my Black womanhood, and everything that means or doesn't mean.

For years women in the Feminist movement and NOW have fought to be heard. "Women's work" and "women's issues" were invisible to the public fifty years ago. The work that NOW and other feminist organizations have done for women is tremendous. But historically the women who profited from feminist organization's work have been White women. In the LGBT community, feminist and LGBT rights organizations have done so much work on the issues that affect White folk in that community, but not focusing on the fact that Black Trans-Women are the poorest group in our country, and are the most likely to face violence and harassment. Even in movements that were supposed to create equality for everyone, People of Color have fallen by the wayside. Told to choose a cause and shut up. Told that others need to win first in order for everyone to win. This was shown to be untrue.

Black women were the ones who pioneered a new meaning of feminism. An intersectional feminism, that truly fights for everyone. NOW in the last few years changed its mission statement to not only include this feminism, but to make it one of the core tenets of the organization. Feminism fights, as renowned feminist theorist bell hooks states, "sexism, sexist exploitation, and oppression."

Sexism doesn't just hurt women, but it hurts men by stereotyping men as killers, specifically Black men as killers and demonizes them. Sexism is already an intersectional oppression. It has affected folk in different ways and on different layers of oppression and privilege. If we are truly fighting for all people to be equal then we must also fight on multiple fronts. We can't forget, Black women and Black transfolk are being killed too. We must fight sexism, racism, transphobia, ableism, classism, and more. As bell hooks writes in the very first line of her book, "Feminism is for Everybody," "Simply put, feminism is a movement to end sexism, sexist exploitation, and oppression," Because of the history of racism Black men have been turned into uncontrollable demons that need to be shot down. Latina women have been turned into one dimensional sexual objects who can't say no, even when they've said no. The undeniable factor of sexism is deeply entangled in racism. So if we truly want to fight ALL sexism, we also have to fight racism.

This all brings me back to the Thursday morning that I woke up with my home in the news. That morning I thought, how could someone mistake a man with a four year old girl in the back seat as threatening enough to shoot, threatening enough to kill? How, if not by seeing the man's sex and race as indicators of difference that brought about fear? Sexism and racism are what turn twelve year old boys who are playing on a playground into dangerous men then into lifeless bodies. Sexism and racism is what brought me to a protest that Thursday night, pounding on NOW signs, yelling and screaming, "No Justice, No Peace," and "Black Lives Matter." Because if we truly are going to fight sexism, and if we are truly going to achieve the goals of Feminism and equality, this is what a feminist needs to look like.

1. The author claims that all too often, feminism has only brought forth positive results for white, heterosexual women. Do you think this is still the case?

2. Does this article broaden your conception of feminism? If so, how?

"LESSONS FROM SLUTWALK: HOW CALL-OUT CULTURE HURTS OUR MOVEMENT," BY ALYSSA TEEKAH, FROM *HERIZONS*, FALL 2015

SlutWalk was born in 2011 in response to remarks made by a Toronto police constable who cautioned students at an under-attended York University safety forum: "I've been told I'm not supposed to say this, however.... Women should avoid dressing like sluts in order not to be victimized." Constable Michael Sanguinetti apologized later for his remarks. However, after the *Toronto Star* wrote about the incident, many more people than the 10 who attended the safety forum learned what the constable had said.

Many women in Toronto were outraged. It wasn't simply the constable's remarks that incensed them. On university campuses across Canada—and, in fact, almost everywhere else—women are commonly blamed for rape, while perpetrators responsible for the crime are unlikely to be held accountable.

Sanguinetti's comments became a tipping point, and a group that included a few York University students, as well as other Toronto feminists, held a protest. They called it SlutWalk in response to the idea that women invite rape by the way they dress. Soon, SlutWalk grew into a global movement in opposition to the slut-shaming and victim-blaming that are endemic to rape culture all over the world. It ignited a new generation of feminist protesters, and more than a million women marched in SlutWalk protests held in many countries, including India, Brazil, Singapore, Israel, South Korea, Poland, the U.K., Australia, Canada and the U.S.

By many accounts, SlutWalks were spontaneous, empowering events for those who attended them. SlutWalk has also had its share of critics, and a new book on the SlutWalk movement by Demeter Press, *This is What a Feminist Slut Looks Like: Perspectives on the SlutWalk Movement*, looks at SlutWalk from all sides.

This article is based on a chapter by Alyssa Teekah, one of the founders of SlutWalk Toronto and one of the book's editors. It captures her reflections on the criticism levelled at SlutWalk organizers by other feminists and outlines the effects of call-out culture on the women's movement.

Four years ago, a group of women, including me, organized what would become the first ever SlutWalk. Today, that experience has taught me a lesson about how we are all capable of both great and not-so-great things—sometimes within the same instance.

My reflections begin with call-out culture—the way that current, heavily Internet-based feminism can turn into a process of publicly shaming people who do not enact the most foolproof politics. Call-out culture is a veritable shark tank, one in which online feminism can become a never-ending, cyclical critique—an unwanted child of intersectionality theory. It's often paired with an impulse to name all of your social locations and to have this naming suffice as your anti-privilege activism.

The champions of intersectional theory would likely be shocked to learn about this dastardly interpretation of their theory, which was originally meant to broaden historical white feminism. In this interpretation, intersectionality becomes ironic—so static that we can fail to see fluidity and diversity. By focusing inward and maintaining analysis at the level of the self, call-out culture obfuscates the larger structures that implicate all of us. What "you" have done wrong to "me" becomes more important than those larger structures.

In academia, students are often taught through a process of critiquing what is problematic about a given work, resulting in a race to be the first to cry out against what's wrong with an act. This quick-to-judge attitude is found in organizing as well, creating a hyperconsciousness that can reduce the space and time for creating new acts.

Regardless of how one has learned feminism, the omnipresence of online feminism reifies these call-out tendencies. The mechanics of blogging, where users can "share" and "follow" particular posts or authors, results in a loop where some content rises and becomes gospel, an exercise in who can shout the loudest. The most bombastic critique is king, and content is shared with the same juicy fervour as celebrity gossip.

While critique is necessary and important, a problem occurs when an entire argument is made up *only* of negative critique. There is no room for both the positives and negatives, or for complexity, and single-track thinking is preferred over nuance. Mired in toxicity, this process of critiquing conflates single moments with the entirety of a person, resulting in an "excommunication" that works in ways similar to practices of public shaming. Nobody is good enough, and overwhelmingly, the message conveyed is that folks should not organize unless they get it right. One is in the position of proving oneself "good enough" for the "movement," and yet one could never be, at least not by call-out culture's standards.

These ideas pervade some arenas of feminism today. We can access a plethora of knowledge, interact and create our own feminisms like never before. Yet, through the same measure, this may mean going through trauma, a twisted rite of passage involving being shamed for comments, arguments or questions that are short of "acceptable" levels of awareness and/or education; one can be torn down to the point of needing to rebuild. We may rebuild, keeping that sense of shame as memory, or we may choose to exit feminism and feminist organizing for fear of being re-traumatized.

The reactions to SlutWalk serve as a strong example of how call-out culture plays out. I identify as a queer, brown (mixed South Asian roots), fat woman with middle-class privilege, graduate-level formal education, relative able-bodiedness and Canadian citizenship status. All of these various social locations factored into my experiences as a co-founder of SlutWalk Toronto.

In the aftermath of the first ever SlutWalk, the feminist and mainstream Internet started to take a bite. We were called out as being colonial when SlutWalk entered other countries, despite the fact that local women had brought the idea in, and not us. We were called out as immature and petty, ignorant and redundant. Older white western feminists seemed to yell at us from their self-imposed pedestals, decrying the shame SlutWalk apparently brought to *their* legacies. We were called insulting and sexist by anti-sex-work feminists, who scoffed at the idea of empowered sexuality. We were called out as idealist and flighty by liberal feminists, who insisted that attention be focussed on economic and capitalist forms of equality.

We were seen as symbolic of the supposed non-legitimacy of social media-based feminism by traditional feminists. We were called elitist by mainstream feminists, who erroneously believed we were all "sheltered university students." Some of the time, these critiques ended up demonizing the very things that had historically been considered part of a feminist worldscape (such as access to education). Mired in the paradox of these critiques, I now understand that they signal a sense of impossibility in doing feminism well. How mundane it is that a movement consisting primarily of women-identified people would make its own feel that they were not good enough.

How have we re-articulated some of the worst violence that patriarchy produces?

It was the other critiques, however—particularly around race—that held more weight for me, given my own intersectionality. The lack of analysis on disability, sex-worker solidarity and the police industrial complex was important, too. A transnational analysis that tied SlutWalk into a global understanding of patriarchy and marginalization would have been critical. All these things exploded and challenged my analyses in ways that I am thankful for today.

The critiques came as a crashing wave that knocked us down. We were hearing it from all sides. Some were silly, but many of them were valid—and there were just so many. Every hour there were new articles, people posting, reposting, tweeting and retweeting critiques. Everywhere I turned, people were shaming, reviling, shitting on SlutWalk. It didn't stop at the level of intellectual critique. It became so overwhelming, seeing hundreds of new posts, messages and articles. Each one, utilizing its shaming language of call-out culture, made me feel smaller and smaller.

On both sides—those critiquing and those receiving—no communication was truly happening. Ugliness reared its head. Instead of pausing and aiming to practise any sort of feminist ethic to discuss what needed to be worked on, white, straight, middle-class and otherwise privileged feminists (who could not see the point of marginalized naysayers) dismissed the critiques of Slutwalk with comments like, "Oh! Those are haters! They are just trying to divide us! They don't get the message!" In these cases, privilege and feminism colluded to create a shield of denial.

One has to develop a thick skin to cope with a culture that actively harms through constant critique. The sad part is, by ignoring the words of the most marginalized, many SlutWalk critics were reproducing the same kind of harm one would expect from oppressive groups.

Call-out culture has built within it its own undoing, in that we develop scars from experiencing its wrath, which actively creates barriers to creating positive change. There was no saving of SlutWalk in this trauma-producing feminism. It was thrown out, baby with the bath water. It felt like everyone started to singularize SlutWalk as a white-supremacist, ableist, homophobic, cis-gendered act. While these characterizations reified those systems of violence, they were rendered as *only* indicative of those systems, and nothing else. SlutWalk was seen as worthless. It was terrible, it was horrible, it was embarrassing and stupid.

And so, by proxy, were the SlutWalk organizers and participants. Our inboxes started filling up. Hate mail. Death threats. People reviled us. It wasn't a process of critique anymore. It was a full-out damning. People wanted us dead. People wanted us to disappear. It was an unforgettable thing to see in writing. It was hard to remember that it was a critique of a specific action we had done, because so much of the critique focused on and questioned our internal selves. On the SlutWalk Facebook group, people who held important, real and necessary anti-racist views went from active participation to experiencing a furious flooding, a barrage of posts, comments and non-stop activity. It was a public shaming, laying waste to every part of us.

Acts we had never committed were ascribed to us, as the fury grew stronger. The lines started to blur between critique and assumptions, critique and falsities. Call-out culture is set up in a way so that folks could not oppose the most vocal critiques. A commenter saying "This critique feels like we are being a little strong—we can do this with kindness or basic respect" would get the response, "You're just as bad as them!" The arguments moved so fast and became vile. I remember trying to engage in a conversation about racism and SlutWalk with a few brief comments. I was obliterated. At the time, I didn't understand the theoretical, practical and historical nature of white supremacy, nor its material and symbolic effects in the ways that related to the effects of SlutWalk.

I was hurt and felt ashamed. These people who were queer, brown and radical—people who should be my community—were calling for my head. It hurt more, and compounded differently, for those organizers who were white. It was harder to place myself within it all, and this made it more confusing to defend myself. This struck me raw. At first, I tried to defend. But then I stopped. And listened. And I realized that much of what they were saying was right. While many of the criticisms were valid, they felt cruel nonetheless. I stand by my belief that the way call-out culture lets people know they could have done better can feel violent. This is what leaves trauma.

I began to engage in measures to distance myself and to dismiss what had happened—enacting the action that follows shame. I stepped down. I left SlutWalk. I watched, and read, and took in the stream of critiques that came, steeping myself in them. I came to understand completely where the critiques were coming from. But, on a personal level, I wasn't sure how I could reconcile my participation in SlutWalk and also understand the critiques.

I was told I had failed, and I wasn't sure where to go from there. So I stayed entirely away. I didn't engage in community. I dropped out of any activist projects I had planned. I felt uncomfortable going to events for people of colour and queer folks. I felt that they knew who I was and would find me unredeemable. I was terrified they would find me out.

Sometimes I would get really down about it, as though I had kicked myself out of the community before I really got to join. I experienced—and continue to experience—anxiety, and I worried that everyone who was queer and racialized was looking at me in a way where they had decided I'd never be worthy, because, in that one instance, years ago, I didn't have the right knowledge and experience—and thus I can never have it.

A key part of what I'm trying to share is the fact that, although I speak here in past tense, these feelings remain. I am overly cautious about participation and still feel I am unwanted in this community. I have a deepened political analysis and have learned so much, but this is paired with a sustained isolation. That is what a feminism that is forged through trauma feels like. It is living in a paradox of intellectually understanding what is fucked-up in the world, yet struggling to find a way to address it, because the fuckery infiltrates your own method!

The lessons offered from this cruel feminism were rough and plain: Never dare to try and make a change unless you know how to do it right. Never comment on fucked-up things unless you know how to please all with your effort. This lesson not only came from feminists who were of comparable schools of thought as me, but from elders, from those who were staunchly antifeminist, from mainstream observers and everyone in between. It's one thing when outsiders want to make sure you are harmed; it's an entirely differently thing when it's people with whom you thought you were "safe." All the critiques that attacked our person echoed the idea that we were worthy of revulsion, that we were just fools. This shame became part of my feminist upbringing.

Trying to bury my participation in and memories of SlutWalk, however, became a funny thing, because it was completely unavoidable! It would come up in conversations, where I would look away and pretend to fade out. It even came up in a dating situations. I once comforted a male-identified rape survivor who told me of healing through Slut-Walk.

The biggest moment was when SlutWalk came up in grad school, as a case for discussion of white liberal feminism. Reading academic work on SlutWalk was like seeing those swirling thoughts in my head articulated by others. While hesitant and concerned about the day of the discussion, I found myself actively participating, both critiquing and defending SlutWalk. My classmates were surprised when I confessed to my participation and were intrigued that I could take this nuanced stance. I realized the freeing dimension of being able to perform a rigorous feminist engagement that could still save some grace and respect for the effort.

After occasions like these, I realized that I could, and did, have pride in SlutWalk after all, and that this was okay. I didn't have to feel ashamed, or bury it: Rather, I could admit it as part of my wider story, of when I was younger and newer to politics. My first experience just happened to be a 3,000-plus-person march. It was a thing that did some good, and some bad, but it was still something I had helped to create. And it was a pivotal moment in modern feminist movements.

1. Do you find "SlutWalk" problematic or offensive? Or do you think this advocacy movement effectively raised awareness towards rape culture? Or both?

2. Do you agree with the author's observations about how call-out culture discourages some from sharing their views for fear of having "imperfect" politics?

"THE CONSERVATIVE ANSWER TO FEMINISM," BY REBECCA NELSON, FROM *NATIONAL JOURNAL DAILY*, MAY 6, 2015

The question that most exasperated Mindy Finn, she says, came from all sorts of people--friends, family, old classmates.

"How can *you* be a conservative?"

People were apparently surprised, the 34-year-old GOP campaign veteran and digital strategist says, that a thoughtful, well-educated woman—she got her bachelor's at Boston University and her master's at George Washington—would freely associate with the Republican Party.

"There's kind of this tendency of viewing conservative women as stuck in the past, I think particularly when it comes to the workplace, and that's just so far from the reality that we're seeing," Finn says. The conservative women she knew were smart and strong and dynamic, and valued a successful career just as much as having a family, she says.

So she set out to combat the negative stereotypes.

Empowered Women, the nexus of that effort, launched in April after months of collaboration with prominent women in politics, business, media, and other industries. The nonprofit seeks to change the prevailing stereotype that conservatives are predominantly old men, pushing back on Democratic charges that Republicans are waging a "war on women," as well as the notion that liberals have a monopoly on women's issues. And it hopes to fill the void of right-of-center women's voices in politics, policy, and culture—helping to foster a conservative alternative to feminism, which Finn says has become a "toxic" term.

"We are absolute advocates for women's opportunity and success," says Finn, who worked on George W. Bush's and Mitt Romney's presidential campaigns before a two-year stint leading strategic partnerships at Twitter. At the same time, she says, the group wants to make sure it's "preserving freedom, family, and free enterprise as priorities."

But stereotypes often stem from truth, and the cliche that Republicans have work to do with women is grounded in reality. Even in 2014, a fruitful election for the GOP, the demographic divide persisted: Women favored Democrats by a 4-point margin, according to Pew, while men preferred GOP candidates by 16 points. Young voters, meanwhile, continued their trend of supporting Democratic candidates.

Empowered Women is trying to alter those trends, starting with a written credo of what the women in the organization believe. The 13 vague, purposefully nonpartisan affirmations include assertions that the group's members are "individuals who think and speak for ourselves" and who "live a fulfilled life, whatever that means to each of us."

From that manifesto, which Finn found tested well with young women across the ideological spectrum, "it was clear there was a need for a sustained effort," she says, one that put bright, influential conservative women in the public eye to dispel the caricatures often touted by liberal rhetoric.

"Seeing is the first step toward believing for many women," says Kellyanne Conway, the president and CEO of the Polling Company Inc./Women Trend, a polling firm in Washington. "And for many women, to see that there's even an alternative to the progressive, liberal orthodoxy that has every woman constantly thinking about abortion, contraception, being a victim of the patriarchy," while at the same time showing "an alternative of fun, engaging accomplished women" helps send that message, she says.

Empowered Women is attempting to build a network of these women across the country. Their April launch, which, in addition to the main event in Washington, included inaugural gatherings in New York City, San Francisco, Los Angeles, Denver, Houston, and Little Rock, drew a slew of conservative women, including politicians on their way up, like freshman Reps. Elise Stefanik of New York— the youngest woman ever elected to Congress—and Barbara Comstock of Virginia.

The organization also plans to conduct research and polling into what college-educated women in their 20s and 30s think and want, and use the findings to shape its messaging and policy aims. Because Empowered Women is a 501(c)3, it won't lobby Congress for specific policies; instead, it will use its research to educate the public about policies its community supports. Along the way, it will encourage the women in the organization's community to speak out, writing op-eds in mainstream media outlets and women's magazines about the cause.

A crucial component of reshaping the conversation around women will be defending against some Democrats' claims that Republicans are anti-woman. That brand of liberal rhetoric backfired in last year's midterms, Finn says, particularly in Colorado, where then-Sen. Mark Udall's strategy of casting Republican challenger Cory Gardner as against reproductive rights—earning the former the nickname "Mark Uterus"—fell flat. Alternatively, Empowered Women seeks to expand the scope of women's issues beyond abortion and contraception.

"That really looks at just a slice of a woman's life: her ability to reproduce, her role, if she chooses, to be a mother," says Leslie Bradshaw, a managing partner at digital product agency Made By Many and a member of Empowered Women's New York City chapter. "It doesn't look at the whole 360 of what it means to be a woman."

What matters to women matters to most voters, the group contends: the economy, national security, health care, immigration. But according to a Pew study from last year, more than half of women voters say abortion is a "very important" factor in deciding who they should vote for.

Still, Finn says that the new generation of conservative women—women in their 20s, 30s, and 40s, Empowered Women's target demographic—has an eye toward "a much broader set of issues" than the women who came before them.

That generation gap indicates a branding problem, says Bradshaw, who used to do political consulting with JESS3, a Washington-based creative agency she founded.

"When people think of 'conservative' and 'Republican,' they think, 'Those are those white guys that make decisions about my body,'" she says. "And that's not the case. That's not this movement."

This effort is distinct from other Republican women-focused groups for that reason, Finn says. Rather than simply provide a place for conservative women to engage each other, or promoting women candidates through PACs like RightNOW Women and Women Lead, Empowered Women wants to lead a campaign to usher in the next generation of conservative women.

"There's been monumental shifts in the last 20 years in terms of women in the workplace, in terms of the makeup of our families," Finn says. "And we want to make sure that our voices and priorities are surfaced so that we're able to align what's being done in the public sphere with what people want."

Lisa Camooso Miller, a partner at public affairs firm Blueprint Communications and former Republican National Committee communications director, says it helps that Finn straddles the Gen X/millennial generation line, because "for so long, the spokespeople for the Republican women have been women that are a generation older than I am," she says.

But more than her age, it's Finn's reputation that carries weight.

"She's well regarded by the moderate women in our party and by the strict conservative women in our party," Miller says. "I think that that's what gives this more promise than maybe any other effort before."

With continuing effort, Finn and her growing network hope to help women feel more confident, assertive, and enterprising. She's reluctant to characterize the organization in terms of feminism, she says, because the word, as tested by her group, has become a lightning rod for controversy.

"I absolutely believe in what feminism is supposed to stand for, which is equal opportunity of the sexes," she says. But Finn, like Madonna before her considers herself more of a "humanist."

And, if Finn and Empowered Women are successful, they hope the incredulity of "How can *you* be a conservative?" will be flipped on its head: "How *can't* you be?"

1. Kellyanne Conway claims that women are tired of liberal's angry focus on abortion rights, and may prefer to be seen as "fun, engaging, accomplished" women. Considering the ongoing war the Republican Party is waging against basic reproductive rights, does this view strike you as trustworthy?

2. Do any of Empowered Women's selling points or insights seem valuable to you, or is this just another attempt to rebrand conservatism as more "woman friendly"?

CHAPTER 5

WHAT THE MEDIA SAY

Has feminism been accurately depicted in the media? Ruth Rosen argues that for thirty years, the answer has been no, and the toll has been enormous. Rosen laments that this fits in with a dispiriting pattern of "American social movements tend[ing] to move from a collectivistic vision to one that emphasizes the success of the individual." In other words, the common trope of women struggling to "have it all" and inevitably falling short undermines the broader goal of feminism—collective struggle for societal transformation. From a media perspective, these articles rarely fail to "stir the pot" and are thus successful click-bait. This journalistic approach obscures how all women must contend with a society that has little socialized resources for support, as well as institutionalized sexism. All too often in the media, feminism's desire to intelligently diagnose and remedy these problems becomes collateral damage in the pursuit of "viral" posts and more clicks.

By contrast, social media networks such as Twitter allow women a forum in which to honestly express the frustrations and contradictions they encounter in everyday life. For this reason, much feminist activism has moved online, and theorizing is happening more informally. Stephanie Taylor discusses how social media acts as a double-edged sword. On the one hand, it allows women to organize, support one another, and bring attention to issues that are difficult to confront on an individual basis, such as surviving sexual assault. Twitter's 140-character limit discourages academic jargon, which some argue is inherently anti-elitist. Taylor recognizes social media's potential, but cautions against the pursuit of a catchy hashtag at the expense of critical thought.

Feminism has also been disseminated via the popular culture of the past decades. In her survey of secondary sources covering the 1990s movement called Riot Grrrl, Virginia Corvid takes us back to a moment in time when a movement could exist, at least in its inception, without the internet. To some, Riot Grrrl's anti-corporate "DIY" ethos and underground fanzine-based culture may appear quaintly out of step with the current moment, one in which mainstream and niche cultures both tend to exclusively lionize popular feminist icons such as Beyoncé.

"WE NEVER SAID "WE WANTED IT ALL": HOW THE MEDIA DISTORTS THE GOALS OF FEMINISM," BY RUTH ROSEN, FROM *ALTERNET*, AUGUST 5, 2012

For over thirty years, the American media have repeatedly pronounced the death of the women's movement and blamed feminism for women's failure to "have it all." But none of this is true. The movement has spread around the globe and early radical feminists wanted to change the world, not just seek individual self-fulfillment.

The latest media-generated debate exploded when Anne-Marie Slaughter revealed in the July 2012 edition of the *Atlantic* Magazine why she had left her fast-track, high-pressured job for Hillary Clinton at the State Department. Families, she admitted, could not withstand the strain. Even a superwoman like herself—blessed with a helpful husband, enough wealth to buy domestic help and child care, could not do it all. Although she described the insane work policies that made her neglect her family, she implicitly blamed feminism for promising a false dream. It was too hard, the hours too long, the persistent sense of guilt too pervasive.

What was missing in her article was the history of "having it all." Too many editors care more about how an article about the death of feminism will, without fail, create a sensation and increase readership than about an inaccurate media trope.

And her article went viral, as they say, setting off a round of attacks and rebuttals about the possibility of women enjoying—not just enduring — family and work. She returned to her former life as a high-powered professor at Princeton University, which in my experience, hardly counts as opting out of trying to have it all.

To Slaughter, I want to say, you may know a great deal about foreign policy, but you certainly don't know much about our history. By 1965, young American women activists in Students for a Democratic Society asked themselves what would happen to America's children if women worked outside the home. Activists in the women's movement knew women could never have it all, unless they were able to change the society in which they lived.

At the August 1970 march for Women's Strike for Equality, the three preconditions for emancipation included child care, legal abortion and equal pay. "There are no individual solutions," feminists chanted in the late sixties. If feminism were to succeed as a radical vision, the movement had to advance the interests of /all/ women.

The belief that you could become a superwoman became a journalistic trope in the 1970s and has never vanished. By 1980, most women's (self-help) magazines turned a feminist into a Superwoman, hair flying as she rushed around, attaché case in one arm, a baby in the other. The Superwomen could have it all, but only if she did it all. And that was exactly what feminists had not wanted.

American social movements tend to move from a collectivistic vision to one that emphasizes the success of the individual. That is precisely what happened between 1970 and 1980. Alongside the original women's movement grew another kind of feminism, one that was shaped by the media, consumerism and the therapeutic self-help movements that sprang up in that decade. Among the many books that began promising such fulfillment for women, was the best seller "Having It All" by Elizabeth

Gurley Brown (1982) who tried to teach every woman how to achieve everything she wanted in life.

Self-help magazines and lifestyle sections of newspapers also began to teach women /how/ to have it all. Both turned a collectivistic vision of feminism into what I have elsewhere called Consumer Feminism and Therapeutic Feminism. Millions of women first heard of the movement when they read about the different clothes they needed to buy in order to look like a superwoman and the therapy they needed to become a confident and competent superwoman. Self-help books and magazines ignored the economic and social conditions women faced and instead emphasized the way in which each individual woman, if only she thought positively about herself, could achieve self-realization and emancipation.

By 1980, the idea of improving all women's lives —sisterhood—had been transformed into creating individual superwomen. Early activists—like myself— bristled at the idea that feminism was about individual transformation. But no matter how many articles feminists wrote, they couldn't compete with all the books and magazines that taught women how to become an assertive, well-dressed independent woman—as long as she had the wealth to hire domestic and child care to assist her ascent into men's world.

In 1976, Ellen Goodman, the late feminist journalist for the Boston Globe, satirized the media's bizarre view of a "woman who had it all:"

"The all-around Supermom rises, dresses in her vivid pants suit, oversees breakfast and then searches for the sneakers and then goes off to her glamorous high-paying job at an advertisement agency where she seeks

Personal Fulfillment and kids' college tuition. She has, of course, previously found a Mary Poppins figure to take care of the kids after school. Mary Poppins takes care of them as if they were her own, works for a mere pittance and is utterly reliable.

Supermom II comes home from work at 5:30, just as fresh as a daisy, and then spends a truly creative hour with her children. After all, it's not the quantity of the time, but the quality. She catches up on their day, soothes their disputes and helps with their homework, while creating something imaginative in her Cuisinart (with her left hand tied behind her back). After dinner—during which she teaches them about the checks and balances of our system of government--she bathes and reads to them, and puts the clothes in the dryer. She then turns to her husband and eagerly suggests that they explore some vaguely kind of kinky sexual fantasy."

The feminist—as remade by the media and popular culture—emerged as a superwoman, who then turned into a scapegoat for a nation's consumerism, the decline of families, and the country's therapeutic culture. For this, the women's movement's was blamed, even though this selfish superwoman who neglected her family seemed bizarre, not to say repellent, to most of the early activists.

The backlash again feminism, directed as it was against the women's movement, reflected a moral revulsion against the shallow self-absorption of America's consumer and therapeutic culture. And when Americans took a good hard look at this narcissistic superwoman who embraced the values of the dominant culture, they grew anxious and frightened. For they no longer saw loyal mothers and wives who would care for their communities, but a dangerous individual, unplugged from home and hearth, in other words, the female version of America' ambitious but lonely organization man. Thus was born the cultural wars between stay-at-home moms and career women.

Anne-Marie Slaughter's article, like most women who have complained about how hard it is to "have it all," focused on an elite group of female professionals who have the means to outsource parts of their job as mother, cook, cleaner and caretaker of the home. What she and others have failed to understand is that the original women's movement sought an economic and social revolution that would create equality at home and at the workplace. Nor have most critics of feminism understood that the so-called "Mommy Wars"—battles fought between those who worked outside the home and those who were "stay-at-home" moms—have also been fueled by the media.

Missing from the media's coverage of these Mommy Wars are the millions of working mothers who will never have it all, but still must do it all. Millions of women cannot afford to care for the children they have, work dead-end jobs, and cannot begin to imagine living the life of a super-woman. These are the women that the radical women's liberation movement addressed and for whom they sought decent jobs, sustainable wages, and government training, social services and child care. These are the women who are stuck on the sticky floor, not held back by a glass ceiling.

1. According to the author, how did the so-called "mommy wars" begin?

2. Why does the author critique Anne-Marie Slaughter's article?

"#FEMINISM: CRITICS OF SOCIAL MEDIA SAY IT'S NOTHING BUT WHITE NOISE—BUT IT CAN ALSO AMPLIFY WOMEN'S VOICES," BY STEPHANIE TAYLOR, FROM *THIS MAGAZINE*, MARCH 16, 2015

Antonia Zerbisias walks into the newsroom, on what is her second last day before retirement. It's early evening on October 30, 2014, and somewhere in between saying some of her last hellos and goodbyes to colleagues at One Yonge Street and attending to whatever final bits of business a columnist and writer has left after more than 25 years at the Toronto Star, she types out a tweet: "It was 1969 when, if you found you were the only girl in the rec room and no parents were home, it was your fault"

Period.

Then, "#BeenRapedNeverReported." Send.

Minutes later, two more tweets, divulging memories that time couldn't erase after 40 years.

" ... 1970: My friend's friend from out of town 'forgot his wallet' in his hotel room ..."

Period. "#BeenRapedNeverReported." Send.

" ... 1974: A half-empty 747 to London. Traveling alone. Fell asleep ..."

Period. "#BeenRapedNeverReported." Send.

Hours before sending out these tweets, Zerbisias was messaging back and forth with long-time friend and Montreal Gazette justice reporter Sue Montgomery, together fuming over public reaction to the women who were then, for the first time, coming forward with their allegations of abuse against CBC's former golden boy radio host, Jian Ghomeshi.

Zerbisias and Montgomery had watched, stunned, as the subsequent flood of questions on Twitter, Facebook, and the comment sections of online articles came in from coast-to-coast: Why didn't the women report anything when it first happened? Why were they only coming out now?

The victim-blaming narrative infuriated both women, and Montgomery suggested they start a list with the names of women who had been raped but had never reported it—just to prove a point. She wanted to do some-thing to "remove the fucking stigma" and get people to speak up and act up. Zerbisias agreed, suggesting they use social media to get their message out far and wide, landing on the hashtag: #BeenRapedNeverReported.

And so, at 2:55 p.m. she sent out her first tweet:

"#ibelievelucy #ibelievewomen And yes, I've been raped (more than once) and never reported it."

Period.

"#BeenRapedNeverReported." Send.

"The rest is history as they say," Zerbisias says with a laugh over the phone from her home in Toronto one evening in January.

Three months after co-creating the hashtag that ignited a global conversation on why women don't report rape, the describing word Zerbisias still uses over and over again is "overwhelmed."

"I didn't decide to start anything. It just happened. The time was right," she says. "It seems to me that all we've been talking about on social media for the past two years is rape. That's what focus of feminism is today. Much of the third wave, as it were, is about rape rage."

"Social media is not just another way to connect feminist and activist voices—it amplifies our messages as well," Jessica Valenti told *Forbes* magazine in 2012. Valenti is a columnist with the U.S Guardian and founder of Feministing, a feminist pop culture website, who, among other accolades, has been credited with bringing feminism online. Indeed, it seems today women's voices are often heard loudest through our screens—a trend some are calling "hashtag feminism." Although the term itself may be debatable, the phenomenon it points to is not: #Bringbackourgirls, #WhyIStayed, #WhyIleft, #YesAllWomen, #YouKnowHerName, and #BeenRapedNeverReported.

Odds are if you're a Twitter user, or at all savvy to social media, you've come across these hashtags. Each was born out of public outcry in the wake of high-profile tragedies: The kidnapping of over 200 Nigerian girls by militant rebels Boko Haram; Janay Palmer's decision to stand by hubby NFL running back Ray Rice after he knocked her unconscious in an elevator; the publication ban on Rehtaeh Parsons' name; and the Elliot Rodger shooting rampage at the University of California campus in Santa Barbara. These hashtags were quickly taken up by millions around the world as outraged rallying cries for change—for women to raise their voices in unison and scream "enough is enough."

Historically, feminists did this by marching and picket lines, staking out their causes with signs and speeches.

Today many are turning their campaigning efforts toward the most public of public spheres: social media. But what's the point of it all? When feminists grab their phones and type out an 140 character message, does it inspire positive change? Do these virtual mantras carry actual power?

Answering the questions surrounding the legitimacy of hashtag campaigns begins with a look back at the very roots of feminism, says Emily Lindin, founder of The UnSlut Project—a multimedia initiative working around cyberbullying and slut shaming. Social media most obviously lends itself to a spirit of solidarity between women, and speaks to the idea of a globalized sisterhood, hardly a new idea to the movement at all.

Lindin says the power of hashtag feminism lies not only in the content of a message, but the number of times that message is retweeted. Within the act of using a hashtag is a real sense of unity, or as Lindin so eloquently puts it: a way to "add your voice to a chorus."

"It's easy but impactful," she explains to me one night in a phone call from California. "Feeling that you're part of something, part of a movement; you're not just feeling that way—you really become part of it." Take the campaign she launched in the fall of 2014, #Okgirls. The hashtag originated from news that three high school girls from the city of Norman, Okla., alleged to have been raped by the same boy at their school, and, unfortunately to no one's surprise, felt abandoned by the school and larger community once the word broke.

Lindin wanted her campaign to create solidarity for the three girls to connect with a globalized network of other sexual assault survivors—to reach out to the young women who had, unwillingly, opened themselves to bullying and potential triggers, just by being online. After all, as Lindin says, one of the hazards created by merging social media and feminism is the vulnerability of opening yourself to trolls, which at best means a slew of derogatory comments, slander, and hate speech. At its worst: death threats, which Lindin herself has experienced. "It works in the way that terrorism works," she says. "If you speak out we attack you and we threaten you so just stop. Don't speak up."

Thinking of the Oklahoma girls, Lindin devised a plan. After contacting the mothers of the girls who had already began the hashtag #YesAllDaughters, Lindin created #Okgirls and asked people to use the hashtag to write direct messages of support and encouragement to the girls using Facebook and Twitter.

"For the #OKgirls: I was raped and then bullied in high school too. You are not alone. I stand with you. #survivor"

"#OKgirls: There is immutable, unmistakable power in your voices. Hear ours too: We believe you. It's not your fault. Now, #NotOneMore."

"#OKgirls: Your voices are strong, brave, clear. It's okay to sometimes feel afraid, but know that there are so many in your corner now."

Lindin then collected these, and hundreds of other similar tweets and curated them into a set of emails—partly to weed out the nasty comments, but also to allow the girls to remain offline and take a break from watching their own stories blown up in headlines and news stories. She emailed the girls' mothers the lists of these tweets, which line after line, read as statements of commitment from survivors and allies to stand up and stand by the three girls as one unified community. "It was amazing," says Lindin.

In January, 2014 Maisha Z. Johnson sends a tweet criticizing her former high school in California. The school had made headlines after spectators at a basketball game chanted, "USA, USA, USA," to a Pakistani student while he stood at the free-throw line. Almost three hours later she's calling out her online harassers with hashtags #OhYouMadHuh #WhyYouMadAboutJusticeTho. As evening rolls on, she switches her focus to a less serious subject matter: "The moon is gorgeous right now! I can't stop staring at her."

Twitter is all about expression; a space for free thought to abound, no matter how minuscule, seemingly insignificant, obnoxious or profound. The phenomenon of status updates in social media offers a moment-by-moment transference of information from "real life" to whomever is behind a screen in a near instant. A point Johnson, a American-writer-activist-poet-turned-social-media-expert unintentionally proves through her own Twitter account, which is that the platform acts as a global space for women to express what she calls their "lived experience"—uncensored and unfiltered.

"I'm not asking for anyone else's permission for what I tweet," she says. "I'm not making sure I have the right terminology or anything like that, I'm just expressing myself." That relationship between terminology and self-expression is pivotal and oftentimes problematic. Too often, Johnson says, people, particularly women, are pre-occupied with finding the right wording to describe and define their own experiences and, as a result, remain silent. It's easy for elitism and academia to dominate conversations about why a woman struggled to find an abortion clinic in her home province with vocabulary like "privilege" or "social transformation." Twitter, says Johnson, brings us back to our "real selves".

Real language can be used to connect with people, rather than being stuck in a bubble of academics—people who, says Johnson, may have all the vocabulary, but aren't necessarily committed to communicating about the everyday.

Criticisms of hashtag feminism cover an array of understandably troubling aspects of digital culture that threaten to undermine the well-intentioned changes of social justice work: the temptation to make a hashtag go viral, for example, by picking a sensationalist message for the sake of garnering more attention, or even the inherent privilege associated with owning a smart phone, which raises questions of access and barriers to technology.

Freelance writer Meghan Murphy also writes on her own blog, Feminist Current, that hashtag campaigns give rise to the invention of the "feminist celebrity," by invariably providing more visibility to certain perspectives on the grounds of popularity while silencing other more marginalized voices, which, in turn, she argues, erodes the very ideology of unity within the movement itself.

However, the most dangerous effect of hashtag feminism seen by Johnson today lays in the constraints of the 140 character limit. The threat: Over simplification. Take the issue of domestic violence, which Johnson herself advocates around in her own writings. On its own, the term, "domestic violence," evokes images of a cis-man, presumably a husband, assaulting his wife, a cis-woman.

What happens to everyone else—LGTBQ folk—who do not fit into this normative understanding of a relationship? How can we communicate the dynamics of violence in an abusive same-sex or trans relationship, such as the fear of being "outed" by a threatening partner under a single blanket term, "domestic abuse"? And how do we do that surrounded by so many other social media campaigns against spousal abuse? The problem is we often can't—well, at least not right away.

Johnson believes Twitter is an entry point for inevitably larger, more contextualized conversations. It is a tool designed to stay informed and get in the know about what's happening, as well as to find the right language to talk about or express an issue.

Lindin agrees. Twitter should be recognized as a chance to jump aboard an idea, she says, not ignite any form of back-and-forth exchange. The 140 character limit is plenty to declare, "here I am," and add your voice to a cause, but there is a deficiency to expound on the nuances of a topic.

"I told my boyfriend and he called me a whore. Broke up with me. #beenrapedneverreported."

"The first question the police asked was, 'what were you wearing?' 1 was 10. #beenrapedneverreported <3"

"I've #BeenRapedNeverReported because I knew I would be blamed because I had been drinking."

By the time Zerbisias went to sleep on the night of October 30, 2014, the hashtag was trending in the U.S. By morning she was receiving emails from American and European media asking for interviews. Four days later, the hashtag was translated into French—and who knows how many other languages since. "I was thrilled because it meant women were not allowing themselves to be re-victimized," she says. "That they were saying 'fuck you,' I'm gonna say this."

The hashtag gave women and men the power, space and freedom to come out and reclaim their attack, declaring that they were indeed raped like so many, many others. It was exhilarating to watch, Zerbisias recalls.

Yet, she refused most of the interviews, and turned down offers from organizations and advocacy groups asking her to get involved with their projects. "That's not my responsibility," she says. "I'm a writer, I'm not a social worker, I'm not a jurist, I'm not a policy maker, I'm not a law maker, I'm not even an organizer."

Headlines from around the world applauded Zerbisias and Montgomery for inventing the hashtag that ignited a global discussion into why 90 percent of women never report their sexual assaults to police. "The question," says Zerbisias, "is, 'What next?'"

1. Why might online activism through social media appeal to many younger people? What are its positive effects?

2. The article identifies a few downsides of this so-called "hashtag activism" such as limited access for some, and the temptation to solicit attention through sensationalism. To what extent do these problems weaken this approach to activism, in your opinion?

"A MANIFESTO FOR ALL: BISEXUAL TRANS ACTIVIST AND AUTHOR JULIA SERANO WANTS TO MAKE FEMINISM INCLUSIVE," BY MARCIE BIANCO, FROM *CURVE*, SEPTEMBER/OCTOBER 2016

In 2007, when Julia Serano's *Whipping Girl: A Transsexual Woman on Sexism and the Scapegoating of Femininity* was published, there was no trans visibility in mainstream culture. Nearly a decade later, upon the book's reissue, trans visibility and issue awareness have reached a cultural apex, thanks to media and entertainment figures like Caitlyn Jenner, Janet Mock, and Laverne Cox. No one, especially bisexual trans activist and author Serano, could have imagined such progress for the trans community. It is for this reason that Seal Press published a second edition of the acclaimed trans-feminist book.

Named No. 16 on Ms. magazine's list of "100 Best Non-Fiction Books of All Time," *Whipping Girl* is one part theory, one part cultural studies, and one part personal essay that argues for a stronger coalition between feminists and trans activists. Back in 2007, long before the current iteration of feminism, Serano contended that we needed a new definition of feminism, one that was inclusive of all genders.

There is an undeniable rift between old-school feminists—Germaine Greer, for example—and the trans community. While it would be easy to call this rift generational, Serano suggests other differences are at the heart of it: "I think that there are a lot of younger trans-exclusionary radical feminists. I would say [the rift] is more philosophical than anything else. If you're entrenched in the idea that sexism is solely encapsulated by the notion that 'men are the oppressors and women the oppressed'—if you have that worldview—then you'll be a lot more inclined to be suspicious of trans people, as well as other various groups, the femme movement or the sex workers' rights, for example."

In *Whipping Girl*, Serano also scrutinizes how misogynistic attacks on femininity similarly affect trans women. "For those of us who move through the world and who 'pass' as cisgender women," Serano explains, "I would say that a lot of the sexism I face since I transitioned is very similar if not identical to what cisgender women face, because people treat me as though I'm a cisgender woman." Misogyny for both cis-gender and trans women stems from how well society reads them as conforming to culturally accepted gender codes.

But many trans women experience an added layer of misogyny in the form of fetishization. Those who do not "pass" face a form of misogyny driven by transphobia, which Serano calls transmisogyny. "Trans women are sexualized in certain ways in our society, where we're seen especially as sexually promiscuous, or that we transition for sexual reasons. There's also the fact that as soon as people know I am trans, there's the possibility that they will decide to not take my identity seriously. In the book, I talk about transmisogyny as being the intersection of transphobia and misogyny, and I think those are always at play when people try to undermine me, if they find out I am a trans woman."

While grateful for the visibility provided by figures like Jenner, Serano believes that the media needs to more thoughtfully consider and represent women, whether cisgender or transgender, who are not paragons of femininity. "Completely absent is any discussion about the average person's gender expectations—the way in which they are very binary, the way in which we view men and women as completely different, and the way in which we encourage people to be gender-conforming and discourage people who are gender-nonconforming. These seemingly minor events," she concludes, "are the root cause for the reason that trans people face so much discrimination in society."

She attributes the broad and rapid change in trans visibility to technology, which she also credits with helping isolated queer kids to connect with one another for support and community. "When I was a kid, going through what I was going through, I went to my local public library and couldn't find any books. At my college, there were three psychology books that were awful and only one trans memoir ... Nowadays, people who are gender-questioning can just get on the Internet and immediately have access to information and to organizations that can help create online communities." When she was young, she says, "Trans communities were very much characterized by isolation. Today we are able to find one another and organize with one another in ways that just weren't possible at the time."

While there is some discussion about the inclusion of the T in LGBT, statistically, it's the B—bisexuals—who are the largest percentage of the LGBT community, and are erased and disrespected by the community. Serano feels that "the T has leapfrogged over the B, insofar as there are a lot of conversations about trans issues, whereas bisexuality is still seen as suspect within the queer community, and this sentiment isn't really much different from what it was 10 years ago."

Serano herself now identifies as bi; a decade ago, she split from her female partner, with whom she was in a monogamous relationship, and began to explore her attraction to men. "I know that for a lot of cisgender women who identify as lesbian for a long time and then start coming to terms with their attraction to men, it can be really difficult to come to terms with identifying as bisexual. For me, I felt it was another way in which I didn't neatly fit into queer women's communities."

She believes that the first step in making bisexuals feel accepted is to acknowledge that they exist; trite generalities like "bisexuality is just a phase" are myths that perpetuate bigotry. But when pressed on how to make bisexuality visible without any verbal declaration, Serano agrees that it is challenging to do so, yet says that to counter biphobia we must collectively resist placing people in the binary of "straight or gay." There is a tendency to make assumptions about a person's sexual preference based on the gender of their partner, rather than on their own chosen sexual orientation.

"I think that dichotomy inherently erases people who are bisexual," says Serano. "It is a binary that we don't talk about as much as we do the gender binary, but it is out there and it does do work erasing people who have non-monosexual sexualities."

At the same time, there is an increasingly prevalent concern within the queer community about "lesbian erasure." Serano herself perceives that "the word 'lesbian' right now is in the same space as 'bisexual' in the larger community." They exist on the margins of the larger LGBT community.

Having gone from identifying as lesbian to identifying as bisexual, Serano offers her thoughts on this concern.

"I am well aware of people who suggest that their lesbian identity, especially butch identity, is disappearing—that there are all these young people who might have identified as lesbian but who now identify as trans, or who have chosen to transition now but would've been lesbian in the past. I think that in different periods in time there are different options for people," she says. "A lot of queer women who were of my Gen X cohort definitely went out of their way to identify as 'queer' or 'dyke' as a way to create some generational distance between themselves and the previous generations, who maybe held some beliefs that the younger generation didn't ascribe to." But for Serano, the notion of "lesbian erasure" is born out of fear and mourning, a sense of loss. Instead, she sees this erasure as "just an evolution in identity labels."

For Serano, the debates—about which letters we include in our acronym, about the community's power hierarchies, its fears and failures—point to a greater need for the entire queer community to have "more conversations about our history." There is a tendency to erase history, and therefore to erase identities, in order to make room for what are perceived as more progressive ideas and identities. Serano disagrees with this revisionism. An "overwhelming majority of us don't have the experience of growing up in our own communities," she says. "We need to find ways to recognize problems that happened in history without necessarily condemning everything that happened in the past ... It's really easy in retrospect to look at those movements and events of the past and say today that they missed the boat, when in fact a lot of the things they did were important."

(juliaserano.com)

1. Why might some radical feminists exclude trans people from feminist discourse? Is this a defensible stance?

2. The author views the community fostered by technology with some ambiguity. Why might social connectivity aid LGBT individuals? Alternately, what might be lost with such easy access to information?

"SOCIAL MEDIA AS A FEMINIST TOOL," BY CONNIE JESKE CRANE, FROM *HERIZONS*, FALL 2012

It's January 2011, and the scene is a safety forum at Toronto's Osgoode Hall Law School. "I've been told I'm not supposed to say this," a Toronto police officer tells a group of female law students. But he says it anyway. Police constable Michael Sanguinetti's next bit of safety advice to the group was, "Women should avoid dressing like sluts in order not to be victimized."

The blame-the-victim riff, from a police representative, no less, touches off a firestorm that would have been hard to imagine before social media. Heather Jarvis, a co-founder of what became SlutWalk Toronto, heard about Sanguinetti's comment on Facebook.

"I was livid when I heard about it," she recalls, "and unfortunately not very surprised."

Together with Sonya Barnett, Jarvis conceived a protest walk to—yet again—raise the issue of blaming victims for rape. A Facebook page came first, then Twitter action. The movement attracted "a lot of people who have never engaged in activism and protests," recalls Jarvis. SlutWalk Toronto took place in May 2011 and drew about 1,000 participants. May 2012 saw a second annual event, and to-date, according to Jarvis, "over 200 cities around the world and counting have had SlutWalks, or SlutWalk-associated events—all different languages, cultures, contexts. It's astounding."

In 2012, Americans saw a similar "slut" comment and storm. After Georgetown University law student Sandra Fluke advocated for the inclusion of birth control in health insurance at religious institutions (like Georgetown), conservative radio host Rush Limbaugh railed at Fluke on air, calling her a "slut" and "whore." But a Twitter campaign (#FlushRushNow) mobilized quickly and led to a huge exodus of advertisers from Limbaugh's show.

So·cial me·di·a
forms of electronic communication (such as websites for social networking and microblogging) through which users create online communities to share information, ideas, personal messages and other content (such as videos).
--Merriam-Webster

In these social media triumphs, there is a strong feminist message. Slate.com sees a "recharging feminism," and the *New York Times* talks of Fluke and "feminist superstardom." Is it any wonder, then, that feminists (alongside gamers and shoppers) are embracing social media?

Women, as we know, are especially active online. According to statistics compiled by Cisco's Ayelet Baron, "women spend about eight percent more time online [than men]. In 2010, 76 percent of women visited a social networking site, compared to 70 percent of men. Specifically in North America, the social networking reach is 91 percent of women and 87.5 percent of males."

But here's a statistic that adds more context: Boston Consulting Group reports that women "control $12 trillion of the overall $18.4 trillion in global consumer spending." With projections like this, you can see why women are bombarded with pop-up ads for shoes, spa Groupons and the chance to join a gout study. Looked at another way, given the revenues at stake, you can also see why feminists banding together online could get an advertiser's attention.

Jarrah Hodge, editor of the Canadian feminist blog Gender Focus, sees social media as revolutionary. "I think social media has a lot of potential to connect feminists and to mobilize feminists and other progressive activists to resist things in popular culture really quickly and effectively."

For feminism, social media is doing two things. First it's allowing broader access to feminist debates. Julia Horel, blog and community manager for the youth-driven *Shameless* magazine (shamelessmag.com), says, "I guess some of the big conversations in feminism have traditionally happened in the academy, and women's studies courses and that kind of thing. But having conversations, and questions, and arguments on all kinds of things on social media brings it to people who might not otherwise have an opportunity to be engaged."

Or, as Hodge says, "When I was in junior high school and we didn't really have social media, we were still reading teen magazines, but we had no way to connect with other people and challenge those ideas. Whereas we saw recently, with Julia Bluhm—a teen who challenged *Seventeen* magazine to use models that weren't Photoshopped—even though they haven't succeeded yet in that campaign, it's raised a lot of aware-ness." Social media's relative affordability, ubiquity and simplicity, adds Hodge, build inclusiveness. "You don't necessarily have to be a writer; you just have to be able to communicate honestly."

YOUNG FEMINISTS AND SOCIAL MEDIA

Secondly, Hodge says, social media can empower younger feminists. "They tend to have more of a voice online than in some mainstream feminist organizations" and are carv-ing out more space for themselves online.

In her podcast series Tweeting Feminists, journalist Ronak Ghorbani interviewed well-known Canadian femi-nist Judy Rebick who observed, "Very few people my age really understand social media." And yet we see fantastic exceptions. Author Margaret Atwood, a passionate Twitter user, speaks proudly of getting Torontonians railing against library closures. Rebick herself told Ghor-bani regarding social media: "I enjoy it. It's really fun, and I also use it politically—it's very useful politically."

Usually, in discussing social media activism, we hype this brave new world—Grrrl slays corporate dragon. But dig deeper and there's a more nuanced truth—social media with its dizzying upsides, but also a labyrinth-like underbelly. As Jarvis says, yes, SlutWalk co-founders added to a global conversation about violence against women. But they also received "a lot of harassment and threatening and bullying" and "horrible rape threats." So much, says Jarvis, that the group halted commenting on its YouTube site.

Then add sniping criticism from journalists. The *Globe and Mail's* Margaret Wente wrote: "SlutWalks are what you get when graduate students in feminist studies run out of things to do." Feminists also dissed the newbie activists, especially around the use of the word slut. In *The Guardian*, feminists Gail Dines and Wendy J. Murphy wrote, "Trying to change [the term's] meaning is a waste of precious feminist resources." Jarvis feels the media often misrepresent SlutWalks. While participants dressed in all sorts of ways, she says, "Somehow the media kept putting out ... images of two women in bras."

It's also stressful when, as an activist and blogger, you're unpaid but also have a day job. With social media activism, financial challenges are the unsung back story. SlutWalk Toronto is run by volunteers. While Jarvis's detractors tend to be well-paid (think tenured professors and established journalists), activists like her tend to do their advocacy work (blogging, media appearances, organizing) as volunteers. "The last year was one of the most overwhelming and challenging of my life," she says.

Deanna Zandt, a New York-based media technologist and author, is the first to acknowledge that a lack of pay is common for social media activists. "No one has an answer for this," she says, but "there are people who are studying it."

Right about here is where the power and challenges of social media intersect. Anyone who's been involved in social media for a while will be recognize the trajectory— an initial high where possibilities blow your mind, followed by a drift back down to earth.

So can social media be revolutionary? Or, as I sometimes fear, are we about to drown in a tsunami of cat videos, grinning vacation snaps and foaming vitriol? Exploring social media for this article, I'm gaining a renewed appreciation. The caveat? Success online, like offline, requires ingenuity, hard work and some light saber dueling against the dark side.

SOCIAL MEDIA CONSUMERISM

One of the biggest challenges is rampant, ad-riddled consumerism. On the one hand, you have weary activists (not to mention venerable institutions such as the *New York Times*, with its new paywall scheme) trying to make enough money online to survive. Alongside, we're witnessing rising corporate investment. Microblogging platform Pinterest, for example, recently made a $1-billion venture capital announcement.

For some, viability means advertising. The big danger here is losing authenticity via product placement. As one satirical bit from *The Onion* ("Women Now Empowered By Everything A Woman Does") reads: "Unlike traditional, phallocentric energy bars, whose chocolate, soy protein, nuts and granola ignored the special health and nutritional needs of women, their new, female-oriented counterparts like Luna are ideally balanced with a more suitable amount of chocolate, soy protein, nuts and granola...."

Of course, feminists are challenging the woman-as-consumer meme, notes Linn Baran, community outreach and promotions coordinator at the Motherhood Institute for Research and Community Involvement and a blogger at motheroutlaws. blogspot.ca. Baran says feminist blogging carnivals, radical mommy blogs and online petitions are all ways we can challenge the dominant narrative.

If you're skeptical about the power of blogging, talk to Sady Doyle. Today a prominent U.S. feminist writer and activist, Doyle writes about blogs politicizing her. "I suddenly saw more than just dating problems and wardrobe issues: I saw double standards, beauty standards, sexual policing and gender roles. And I began to understand, too, how small those concerns were, and how my obsessive focus on them was intrinsically tied to my privilege."

Online, the trick is to keep your eyes wide open. Baran shares a favourite analogy from Jen Lawrence, whom *Toronto Life* magazine called one of "Toronto's pioneer mommy bloggers." In an essay for the book *Mothering and Blogging: The Radical Act of the MommyBlog*, Lawrence writes, "I think that blogging can be an incredibly powerful tool when it comes to building community, even if there are blog ads running down the sidebar.

"But I don't want blogging to become just another guerilla marketing technique." She offers this analogy: "I don't want to be invited to a friend's home, only to discover I was really invited to a Tupperware party."

THE DOWNSIDE OF SOCIAL MEDIA

Of course, if you're being skewered online by nasty trolls, a Tupperware party could be tempting. Anyone who makes even mildly controversial statements online knows how much venom you can draw, and feminist statements remain lightening rods. The negativity, says Hodge, "can be really demoralizing, especially if you're someone who's new to social media."

Doyle, who launched a Twitter campaign called #MooreandMe after hearing filmmaker Michael Moore call sexual assault charges against WikiLeaks founder Julian Assange "a bunch of hooey," received rape threats for her action. Eventually her campaign wrung an apology from Moore. As she explained in her blog: "I'm being harassed, I'm being threatened, I'm scared for my physical safety to the point that I'm looking up dudes and seeing exactly what stalking consists of in case I have to press charges."

Jarrah Hodge at Gender Focus says bloggers can't rely on hosts to help if contributors receive threats. "Oftentimes, the companies that run the [larger] sites aren't very responsive," she says. Hodge aims to create a safer space for feminist dialogue on her blog by including a comments policy. "I cite reasons why I might remove your post. And I will never let hate speech or really disrespectful personal attacks stand un-countered."

For *Shameless's* Julia Horel, it's all about "deciding what's worth your energy and what's not." Adds Jarvis, "It's sometimes blocking people from pages, removing comments," while accepting that feminist comments will see personal attacks. "You need support around and you need to realize your skin is going to get thicker."

INFORMATION OVERLOAD

Haters, advertisers, your 200 Facebook friends and the 50 blogs you're following—it's a lot to manage. While we see social media's value, there's a growing realization that it can be overwhelming and even addictive. Individuals and organizations are experimenting with boundaries: daily Facebook limits, Internet fasts and device-free weekends. We're just beginning to study what social media have done to us.

Information overload is a huge issue, agrees Joey Jakob, a Ph.D. candidate in communication and culture at Ryerson and York universities. "Social media allow us to have a kind of access we haven't been able to have," says Jakob, who addressed a 2012 conference in Waterloo, Ontario, alongside such luminaries as Margaret Atwood and Jane Urquhart. "Do we even have the time and energy to think about [social responsibility] when we're just continuously overstimulated by continuous knowledge filtering in through social media?" asked Jakob.

"What we don't talk about enough is the actual amount of responsibility" our social media use involves, says Jakob. Consuming social media, Jakob thinks, requires us "to contextualize everything. It can be very tiring, I will admit it, to put everything in context, but I think if nothing else, that's our responsibility."

THE FUTURE

But how do we do this? How do we filter out junk and venom and develop a mindful, positive social media habit? As her recent book title, *Share This! How You Will Change the World with Social Networking*, suggests, Deanna Zandt is optimistic.

We will, says Zandt, learn to better handle the flood of information, and even the haters. "Some women are sort of turning it on their head and creating Tumblr blogs of the hate mail that they receive.... We don't have to be silenced."

Looking ahead, Zandt envisions social media activists continually informing and influencing traditional power hierarchies. In her book, she writes that "the freely available nature of the tools reduces some of the complexity of organizing. We no longer have to rely on the old ways of top-down, or even organization-based, grassroots organizing." She concludes with clear-eyed confidence: "Technology isn't a magic bullet for solving the world's problems, but it's certainly a spark to the fastest fuse to explode our notions of power that the world has seen in a thousand years."

1. Is social media an effective way to organize and exchange information? Or is it overwhelming and distracting? What has been your experience?

2. As a forum for political speech including feminist advocacy, how do you see the balance between social media's power and its potential downsides?

"'VERNACULAR THIRD WAVE DISCOURSE': NEW WORKS ON RIOT GRRRL, GIRL ZINES, AND GIRL ROCK," BY VIRGINIA CORVID, FROM *FEMINIST COLLECTIONS: A QUARTERLY OF WOMEN'S STUDIES RESOURCES*, FALL 2010

DON'T NEED YOU: THE HERSTORY OF RIOT GRRRL. 40 mins. Directed by Kerri Koch. Produced by Urban Cowgirl Productions, 2006. DVD available for purchase: $14.99 plus shipping, **http://urbancowgirlproductions.com/ uc/?page_id=3/**.

Sarah Marcus, *GIRLS TO THE FRONT: THE TRUE STORY OF THE RIOT GRRRL REVOLUTION.* New York: Harper, 2010. 281 p. $14.99, ISBN 978-006180636.

Marisa Meltzer, *GIRL POWER: THE NINETIES REVOLUTION IN MUSIC.* New York: Faber & Faber, 2010. $14.00, ISBN 978-0865479791.

Alison Piepmeier, *GIRL ZINES: MAKING MEDIA, DOING FEMINISM.* New York: New York University Press, 2009. 272p. $22.00, ISBN 978-0814767528.

GIRLS ROCK! THE MOVIE. 89 mins. Directed by Shane King & Arne Johnson. Produced by (Your Name Here) Productions and Ro*co Films International, 2008. DVD available for purchase for home use: $25.00 plus shipping, **http://www.girlsrockmovie.com/order.** Licensing for educational and public showings also available.

Marisa Anderson, ***ROCK 'N'ROLL CAMP FOR GIRLS: HOW TO START A BAND, WRITE SONGS, RECORD AN ALBUM AND ROCK OUT!*** San Francisco, CA: Chronicle Books, 2008. 191p. $14.95, ISBN 978-0811852227.

In the early 1990s, the punk feminist movement called Riot Grrrl emerged in the United States, with hubs of significant activity in Olympia, Washington, and Washington, D.C. Combining musical performance, zine production, irreverent style, and the DIY ethos of punk, Riot Grrrl forged a feminist praxis premised upon social and personal transformation through cultural production and girl community—or, as Riot Grrrl put it, girl love and girl power. Recent scholarship has begun to examine this movement and the larger Third Wave of feminism in which it was located. Simultaneously and with significant overlap, Riot Grrrl participants have begun to document their activities and to foster the empowerment of a new generation of girls. Like Riot Grrrl, these new offerings confront ongoing struggles with intersectionality in feminism and misrepresentation of feminism in the mainstream media. Throughout these tensions, however, the transformative power of women and girls creating culture and critiquing patriarchy remains the touchstone in these vibrant works.

For those new to the history of Riot Grrrl as a feminist musical movement, *Don't Need You*, a documentary film by Kerri Koch, offers an excellent introduction. The film features interviews with the prominent zinesters and musicians, such as Corin Tucker of Heavens to Betsy, Allison Wolfe of Bratmobile, Kathleen Hanna of Bikini Kill, Sharon Cheslow of Chalk Circle, Ramdasha Bikceem of Gunk, and Madigan Shive of Tattle Tale.[1] Koch uses interview footage and archival materials interspersed with excerpts from the Riot Grrrl manifesto originally published in *Bikini Kill 2* to weave the fabric of the narrative.[2] This approach tracks individual experiences of Riot Grrrl, as well as a historical timeline of Riot Grrrl's rise to prominence and subsequent participant disillusionment relating to the movement's primarily white, middle-class participant base and trivialization in the media.

The film closes with reflections on the meaning and significance of Riot Grrrl that recuperatively position it as a feminist movement of young female artists. With this narrative arc and material, Koch's composition not only provides a compelling introduction to Riot Grrrl, but also strikes the sensitive and informed tone necessary for conveying the story of a movement that was ideologically opposed to definition and experienced outside definition as such a negative force. Alongside the documentary, Koch provides extended interview and archival material footage in the bonus features, making the film an even greater resource for further Riot Grrrl scholarship.

For a more indepth examination of the history of Riot Grrrl, *Girls to the Front: The True Story of the Riot Grrrl Revolution*, by Sara Marcus, delivers on its subtitle and offers a singularly comprehensive, multi-faceted account. Marcus brings a unique insider/outsider perspective to Riot Grrrl history. As she reveals at the beginning of the book, Marcus missed the early years of Riot Grrrl development but later connected to Riot Grrrl at a center of activity in Washington, D.C. Therefore, she has an intimate familiarity with Riot Grrrl feminist analyses, but also a distance from the stormiest events in Riot Grrrl's history. From this position, she relays many of the complicated and dispersed strands of Riot Grrrl history based on her familiarity and five years of research. Her account covers the bands Bikini Kill, Bratmobile, and Huggy Bear, as well as Riot Grrrl activity in Olympia, D.C., New York, the Twin Cities, and Omaha. Throughout, the account incorporates interviews, lyrics, and zine excerpts and positions Riot Grrrl in the context of the 1990s backlash, especially anti-abortion politics. As the timeline unfolds, it transitions from the early centrality of punk to the later centrality of zines. The trivializing and sensationalized media fascination with Riot Grrrl and the controversial media blackout also receive indepth coverage. Although other writers have addressed these aspects of Riot Grrrl history before, Marcus brings a new level of detail and temporal development.

Girls to the Front also offers sustained attention to the focus, in Riot Grrrl, on sexual harassment, physical abuse, and sexual violence, which most previous coverage has either glossed, ignored, or actively suppressed. As Marcus demonstrates, the personal experience of these issues motivated many young women and girls to connect to Riot Grrrl in an era when the media was declaring feminism dead. This previously under-addressed perspective emerges from Marcus's innovative narrative style, which grounds her presentation of Riot Grrrl activity in the perspectives of the actors. Contradictory perspectives, analyses, and interpretations receive side-by-side sympathetic telling, yet the overall coherence of the work remains intact and is strengthened by the contradictions. The book would have benefited, however, from more attention to the perspectives of grrrls of color. Although Marcus attends to the predominantly white participant base of the movement and the resistant reaction elicited by an "unlearning racism" workshop at the first Riot Grrrl convention, interviews with prominent grrrls of color like Mimi Nguyen and Ramdasha Bikceem are notably absent. Despite this failing, *Girls to the Front* has much to offer and deepens the extant scholarship on Riot Grrrl.

In another approach, Marisa Meltzer examines Riot Grrrl as an antecedent to the music and marketing phenomena of girl power. She states her intentions in the preface to *Girl Power: The Nineties Revolution in Music*: "In this book I have traced the roots, evolution, and eventual co-option of girl power in an attempt to figure out what it all means and where music and feminism are headed" (p. ix). Meltzer also makes it clear that she intends to focus on privileged perspectives on this history, commenting, "The good feminist in me wants to make sure that I'm not overlooking any outsider groups, but they are not part of the story I am looking to tell" (p. x)— a shortsighted approach, since constructions of white femininity, consumerism, and hetero-sexuality have been at the heart of co-opted definitions of girl power. With this broad, vague research question and self-authorization to downplay or ignore issues like race, class, and sexuality, the slim volume unsurprisingly comes across as hollow. It reads like a series of long expository magazine articles covering, in succession, Riot Grrrl, "Angry Womyn" in rock, 1990s girl groups, 1990s female pop stars (aka "Pop Tarts"), and Ladyfest feminist musical and art festivals.

Girl Power comes across as a thin layer of journalistic coverage stretched over Meltzer's personal grappling with the contradictions between enjoying the consumption of pop culture and her feminist analyses. *Girl Power* taunts the reader. Underneath the pop-culture details, music history summaries, and personal anecdotes lies an enduring feminist debate: female pleasure versus resisting oppression. Without an explicit or coherent take on the debate, though, much of the book's discussion seems arbitrary and based on personal taste: Spice Girls and Brittany Spears: thumbs up. April Lavigne and Pussy Cat Dolls: thumbs down. Both Meltzer and this topic have more to offer than the blog-post-like fare presented in *Girl Power*.

While Meltzer examines Riot Grrrl as part of a larger musical history, Alison Piepmeier, in *Girl Zines: Making Media, Doing Feminism*, addresses the movement as part of a larger development of feminist zines. The first monograph-length academic examination of feminist zines, Piepmeier's work is an insightful and long-overdue engagement with the feminist work in zines, which played a pivotal role not only in Riot Grrrl but also in the development of the Third Wave in general. Piepmeier aptly defines zines as "vernacular third wave" discourse (p. 9), and she combines "the existing scholarly work on zines with a much-needed broad range of interdisciplinary perspectives on book culture, activist art, and participatory media in order to map out as fully as possible the personal, political and theoretical work that grrrl zines perform" (p. 7). Observing that "the third wave has been widely described but undertheorized," Piepmeier suggests that "the theoretical contributions—the vocabulary, conceptual apparatus, and explanatory narratives—of the third wave have not been recognized by scholars because they're being developed in unexpected, nonacademic sites, like zines" (p. 10). The text helps bridge this gap with well-researched examinations of exchange in zine culture, the Third Wave, and the range of constructions of femininity in zines, as well as the handling of intersectionality and revolutionary hopefulness in zines. Comfortable with complexity, Piepmeier critiques binary divisions of victimization/agency and complicity/resistance to develop a nu-anced perspective of the feminist work and discourse in girl zines. Overall, the book admirably engages the complicated nature and context of girl zines, including girl culture, Third Wave feminism, and girl zines themselves whose creators contradict and explicitly resist definition or description (pp. 11-12). This thoughtful and multi-disciplinary examination of feminism in girl zines should be in every collection on zines or the Third Wave.

Rock 'n' Roll Camp for Girls combines Peipmeier's observation that Third Wave theory is developed in "unexpected nonacademic sites" and Riot Grrrl feminist musical practices. Founded in 2000 in Portland, Oregon, by Misty McElroy as a student project, the camp brings together girls aged 8-17 for a week to form bands, choose instruments, write songs, and perform them in a showcase concert. Although music provides the structure for the camp, girl empowerment is the focus. Camp activities include a self-defense workshop from Free to Fight, attention to conflict resolution, and discussions of the representation of women in the media and women's exclusion from musical production. Volunteers teach classes, facilitate the bands and perform music throughout.

The documentary film *Girls Rock!*, directed by Shane King and Arne Johnson, provides an insider look at the experience of Rock 'n' Roll Camp for Girls from the perspective of participants, their families, and staff. Following the girls through an intense and tension-filled week of everything from learning instruments to performing with a group of recent strangers, the footage rivets. Besides presenting the compelling event that the camp is, the film also mirrors the focus of the camp and emphasizes the difficulties girls face with self-esteem and body image. In-depth serial interviews with a selection of camp participants, their families, and staff—including Carrie Brownstein of Sleater Kinney, sts of the Haggard, and Beth Ditto of the Gossip—function as the strengths of the documentary. The directors and camera crew clearly established a rapport. Yet, because the film directors were just learning about the history of women in music and the effects of sexism on girls as they worked on the project, the film has some weaknesses. For instance, although the camp had a diverse staff and participant group, the directors presented a whitewashed version of the history of women in music, and used one-dimensional statistics about girls. More subject expertise on the part of the directors would have enhanced the framing of the film, but the coverage of the camp itself is outstanding and a worthwhile watch.

While *Girls Rock!* provides a window into the experience of attending camp, *Rock 'n' Roll Camp for Girls*, edited by Marisa Anderson, offers a DIY version of the camp in book format, or, as the subtitle puts it, "How to Start a Band, Write Songs, Record an Album and ROCK OUT!!" Its tone is pitch perfect, both accessible and smart, and it's aimed at "anybody who has ever dreamed of playing music" (p. 12). Illustrations by Nicole Georges and photos from camp, rendered in lime-green and black and white throughout and assembled with a cut-and-paste style, create a zine-like feel for the book. Numerous contributors offer advice and directions based on personal experience, including notables Carrie Brownstein of Sleater-Kinney, Sarah Dougher of Cadallaca, Cynthia Nelson of Ruby Falls, Kaia Wilson of Team Dresch, Beth Ditto of The Gossip, sts of The Haggard, and a host of other seasoned musicians, organizers, and writers. As a whole, the compilation combines inspiring essays on women in rock and the artistic process with practical directions on songwriting, instruments, electrified sound, and starting and promoting a band. Sections on self-defense and punk rock aerobics, a glossary of relevant music terms, chord charts, and contact information for rock camps round out the book as a resource for girl musicians. Get it for the girl in your life and support her art.

1. This article traces some recent studies of third-wave feminist popular culture. Do you find this history relevant?

2. Riot Grrrl sought (among other goals) independence from rigid definitions and resistance of monolithic culture in favor of a "DIY" aesthetic. Do these values live on today? Or has popular feminism been co-opted into something too mainstream?

CHAPTER 6

WHAT ORDINARY PEOPLE SAY

Average Americans either misunderstand feminism, or simply reject the term based on its connotations, associations, and impressions, which are not always relevant to what feminism actually entails. According to recent polling, the vast majority of Americans (82 percent) believe that "men and women should be social, political, and economic equals." But when asked if one calls oneself a feminist, these numbers plummet to miserable depths: less than a quarter of American women are willing to identify with the feminist tag, while even fewer men are cottoning to the label. How do we account for this discrepancy between belief, identification, and endorsement? Does feminism have a PR problem? Is it too radical for mainstream America? Or do these numbers reflect serious theoretical grievances with the feminist agenda, as it currently stands?

Not surprisingly, the best answer is probably "all of the above." Regarding millennial women, Denise Cummins argues that the victories won by second-wave feminists have been taken for granted by younger women, who do not experience a blatantly segregated employment market or limited access to higher education. For this reason, they see little reason to embrace feminism. Cummins additionally suggests that many young women disagree with gender feminism's (by no means uncontested) axiom that gender is entirely socially constructed. The irony should not escape us that a theory meant to critique repressive constructions of gender has become a straw (wo)man for relatively privileged women, happy in their traditional roles, to rail against.

Indeed, one commonly held notion is that women cannot identify as a feminist while also embracing traditional feminine roles such as full-time motherhood and domesticity. In her personal narrative, Frederica Mathewes-Green recounts such a journey from radicalism to family fulfillment. Reacting to her perception of misguided negative energy within the movement, Mathewes-Green put her political activism behind her. This basic story will no doubt resonate with many women of her generation, but begs the question as to whether the feminist baby has been thrown out with the bathwater.

It is curious that so few women are willing to embrace by name a movement advocating solidarity and the betterment or their condition, especially considering that equal pay has yet to be achieved in practice, rape culture is pervasive, and Republican lawmakers are hell-bent on controlling women's reproductive systems. It is possible that feminist practice will continue regardless of labels. After all, what's in a name anyway? Unfortunately, it is also possible the Americans are socialized to accept increasingly powerful ideology—ideology that may even work against the best interests and highest aspirations of both women and men.

"COLUMN: WHY MILLENNIAL WOMEN DON'T WANT TO CALL THEMSELVES FEMINISTS," BY DENISE CUMMINS, FROM *PBS NEWS HOUR*, FEBRUARY 12, 2016

How dare they?

Much to everyone's surprise, recent polls show that a significant majority of millennial women plan to vote for Bernie Sanders rather than Hillary Clinton. In response, feminist heavy-hitters such as Gloria Steinem and former Secretary of State Madeleine Albright lost no time in scolding young women for their perceived treachery.

"There's a special place in hell for women who don't help each other," warned Albright at a Clinton rally. On the "Real Time with Bill Maher" show, Steinem suggested younger women were backing Sanders just so they could meet young men. She quipped, "When you're young, you're thinking, 'Where are the boys? The boys are with Bernie.'" (Steinem later apologized.)

Sanders draws strong support from millennials, because he represents to them someone who will solve the problems that most directly impact their lives — student loan debt, free college tuition, better job market. Ironically, they seem to be unaware that Clinton plans to tackle those very same issues, albeit in different ways. They've bought the message that a vote for Clinton is a vote for "the establishment."

And could it be that some women shun Clinton because of competitiveness? This phenomenon, in which women simultaneously hold other women to higher standards, and then penalize them for reaching those standards, often plagues highly successful women. We see this kind of thing all the time in academia, where female professors routinely get lower teaching ratings than their male colleagues, particularly from female students.

But my reading of this phenomenon is more forgiving of millennials. I think their distrust actually represents an indictment of modern day feminism.

Riddle me this: Why do the vast majority of Americans believe in equality for women in the workplace and the home, yet refuse to call themselves "feminists"?

A 2013 Huffington Post/YouGov poll showed that only 23 percent of women and 16 percent of men consider themselves feminists — even though 82 percent of both genders believe "men and women should be social, political, and economic equals."

If this state of affairs does not seem like a contradiction to you, then consider the dictionary definition of feminism: "The belief that men and women should have equal rights and opportunities; the theory of the political, economic, and social equality of the sexes."

Should we chalk up this apparent contradiction as yet another example of human irrationality? I don't think so, for three reasons:

1. THE CURRENT GENERATION HAS RARELY EXPERIENCED INSTITUTIONALLY AND LEGALLY SANCTIONED SEXISM.

First-wave feminists were the suffragettes who fought to give women the vote. The majority of second-wave feminists (like me) were women of the 1960s and 1970s who believed that the rights and privileges of citizenship should not be curtailed on the basis of gender. We acted on these beliefs by fighting to improve women's socio-economic and educational opportunities, and to improve women's access to reproductive health care (such as birth control and abortion). We wanted life to be fairer and better for ourselves and for future generations of women. Philosopher Christina Hoff Sommers refers to these feminists as "equity feminists."

But, ironically, it is the very triumphs of second-wave equity feminism that lead young women to believe feminism has nothing to do with them. They have never faced a world in which employment ads were neatly divided into high-paying "Help Wanted: Male" and low-paying "Help Wanted: Female" categories, where women were forbidden entry into top-tier colleges like Harvard and Yale, where birth control was difficult to get and abortion was illegal. These scenarios sound like science fiction to today's young women rather than descriptions of recent history.

2. THE TERM "FEMINISM" HAS BEEN HIJACKED BY A MINORITY OF VOCAL EXTREMISTS WHO HAVE REDEFINED IT AS "GENDER FEMINISM," CLAIMING THAT GENDER IS A PATRIARCHAL SOCIAL CONSTRUCT CREATED IN ORDER TO OPPRESS WOMEN.

Gender feminism is based on the discredited belief that humans are born as blank slates and all sex differences are artifacts of socialization. They believe the only way to achieve true political and economic equality is to erase all differences between men and women by rigidly socializing boys and girls to be the same.

Gender feminism is very much alive and well in American colleges and universities, housed within many Women and Gender studies programs. And it is there that some young women decide to distance themselves from the term. Barnard College student Toni Airaksinen recently blogged about her experiences in such a program:

> In one year, I took three Women's Studies classes. My professors taught me that, because I was a woman, I was victimized and oppressed. Prior to enrolling, I did not see myself that way … Mentioning anything that didn't support the notion that females were unilaterally oppressed would be akin to blasphemy.

As gender feminists try to inculcate a psychology of victimhood in their students, the progress second-wave equity feminists accomplished is slowly eroding. Planned Parenthood is under attack and was nearly defunded, putting the lives of millions of poor women and their children at risk. Abortion clinics are bombed, and abortions rights are so greatly curtailed that doctors must perform invasive and unnecessary ultrasounds. And women continue to earn less than men in the broader workplace.

3. "FEMINIST" HAS COME TO MEAN "CAREERIST" — COMPETING WITH MEN IN THE WORKPLACE ON MEN'S TERMS.

This implies that stay-at-home mothers cannot be feminists and that women must put career ahead of family in order to compete.

This phenomenon can be traced to a shameful chapter in second-wave feminism. Shulamith Firestone declared "Pregnancy is barbaric." Ellen Willis admitted that "I saw having children as the great trap that completely took away your freedom." Gloria Steinem described her mother as spiritually broken by giving up her career as a journalist to raise her children.

Within the confines of the traditional workplace, where men were the breadwinners and women's place was in the home, careers are meant to be unbroken, rising trajectories. We are expected to claim our turf and prove ourselves in our 20s and 30s and move into positions of greater prestige, power and authority in our 40s and beyond.

This, of course, leaves no room for forming and caring for young families. Hitting the "pause" button in mid-career to raise a family makes it difficult if not impossible to resume one's career later. The time spent raising the next generation of taxpayers and entrepreneurs will be seen as time wasted, and your resume will be deep-sixed for "lack of initiative." Too often, this is true even if "hitting pause" simply means going part-time or requesting fewer travel demands.

To bring this point home, consider the results of the Harvard and Beyond Project conducted by economists Claudia Goldin, Lawrence Katz, Naomi Hausman and Bryce Ward, a project that tracked three cohorts of female Harvard graduates (1970, 1980 and 1990) 15 years after they received their degrees. The striking impact of children on women's careers was apparent. Among those who had no children and a law degree, 83 percent were employed full time. For those who had one child, only 64 percent were employed full time, and for those who had two or more, fewer than half (49 percent) were employed full time. These values were the same for MBAs, PhDs, physicians, dentists and veterinarians.

Goldin explains the wage and career-ladder gap this way: "Quite simply the gap exists because hours of work in many occupations are worth more when given at particular moments and when the hours are more continuous." As Goldin points out, what is needed is a system that rewards the *amount* of work accomplished rather than *when* the work is accomplished. The current system rewards work done early in one's career far more heavily than work done subsequently.

Our double-income marriages had another unforeseen impact on the entire country and economy: a red-hot housing market. According to Elizabeth Warren and co-author Amelia Warren Tyagi, today's two-income family earns 75 percent more money than its single-income counterpart of a generation ago, but actually has less discretionary income once their fixed monthly bills are paid. This is because higher family incomes triggered a ferocious bidding war for housing and education among the middle class.

Housing and tuition prices skyrocketed, which now means that there *must* be two wage earners in the family because it is virtually impossible for families to live a middle-class existence on only one middle-class paycheck.

So this is how we live today, aptly described by William Falk, the editor in chief of The Week:

> As I write this, my wife, Karla, is on a business trip to Chicago, and I am in the 15th hour of a day that began at 6 am ... On days like this, I think back to seeing my successful dad walking home from work nearly every day at 5:30 pm. My stay-at-home mom had dinner in the oven; my brother and I ate with our parents, and we all spent a leisurely evening together. How 20th century. Today, the world is globalized, profit-driven, hyper-competitive; our employers run lean, demanding more and more hours from those of us who haven't been pruned (yet). We must carefully ration any time spent on our kids, our spouses, ourselves. In return for our relentless productivity, our "standard of living" has risen: We get to buy cooler devices, nicer cars, more stuff. We are so much richer and more fulfilled. Aren't we?

Second-wave equity feminists smashed the barriers to greater political, educational and economic opportunities for women. The new challenge for third- and fourth-wave feminism is to take back the term from radical gender feminists and to take back our personal lives from an unyielding workplace.

1. This article claims that millennials believe in feminism, but do not identify as feminists. Is this a problem? If so, why?

2. Is the author's characterization of radical "gender" feminism wholly accurate in your view? Is she missing any important insights arising from women's studies and other more theoretically inclined feminists?

"FEMINISM TODAY: WHAT DOES IT MEAN?" BY KATHY FRANKOVIC, FROM *YOUGOV*, AUGUST 1, 2014

MOST PEOPLE DON'T WANT TO CALL THEMSELVES FEMINISTS – BUT MANY PEOPLE CHANGE THEIR MINDS WHEN FEMINISM IS ASSOCIATED WITH EQUALITY

Just one in four Americans – and one in three women – call themselves feminists today. But that's before they read a dictionary definition of feminism. Even then, 40% of Americans in the latest *Economist/YouGov* Poll – including half of all men – say they do not think of themselves as a feminist, defined as "someone who believes in the social, political and economic equality of women."

Women are more than twice as likely as men to say they are feminists at first, although only a third of women describe themselves that way. The gap remains about the same when people read the dictionary definition. Once that happens, identification increases dramatically: half of men and two-thirds of women say they are feminists.

There are some groups whose members reject the feminist label: 58% of all Republicans say they are not feminists even after seeing the definition. 62% of GOP men say they do not agree with the definition of feminism. So do 46% of GOP women.

Women under 30 seem to have embraced the term – even without a definition. 51% of women under 30 call themselves feminists. So do a majority of higher income and college educated women. 70% and more in those groups say that after reading the dictionary definition.

For many others, however, the term "feminist" is an insult. One in four adults say it is. So do one in three Republicans (40% of GOP men say this).

Attacks on the term by conservative commentators and others may have influenced how those who think the term is an insult regard feminism. Asked for a word to describe it, they most frequently call it "liberal," "stupid" and "misguided."

Just 14% overall say that calling someone a feminist is a compliment. Most Americans think it is just a neutral term. Even those who identify as feminists themselves are divided on whether the term is a compliment or just a description. 44% of feminist women say it is a compliment; 52% say it is neutral.

Those who say "feminism" is a compliment most often use "strong" as the best word to describe it. "Progressive," "determined" and "equality" are also popular. The word cloud for those who see feminism as neutral displays many of the same words as the positive cloud does, though "liberal" and some negative words also appear, but less often than among those who think the term is an insult.

While the use of the term "feminist" divides Americans by party and by gender, there are some areas of wide agreement that show changes over time. In the 1930's and 1940's Americans <u>disapproved</u> of a married woman working if she had a husband who could support her. Those opinions had turned around by 1970, and now, fewer than one in ten Americans say they disapprove of a married woman working outside the home.

15% of those 65 and older disapprove, but that is a small pocket of resistance.

Americans also agree that it is harder to be a mother today than it was when they were children. That is an especially strong feeling among the oldest group, whose childhood was longer ago. 75% percent of those 65 and older believe it is harder to be a mother today than when they were children, something just 43% of adults under 30 agree with (a third of young adults say not much has changed in this regard since they were children, one in four say being a mother is easier now).

But Americans disagree on what a mother with children should be doing. A majority believe that children are better off if the mother stays home with the children and doesn't work. But that percentage is down from last year, when nearly two-thirds agreed.

Men favor women with children staying home by 20 points (60%-40%); women are closely divided (52%-48%). Feminist women disagree by two to one (34%-66%).

1. What do you think so many people avoid the label "feminist" while still supporting some of its essential tenets?

2. Are there any signs from the above survey that America is becoming more progressive on gender?

"IF YOU'RE NOT A FEMINIST – WHAT THE HELL IS WRONG WITH YOU!!?" BY STEVEN SINGER, FROM *COMMON DREAMS*, SEPTEMBER 10, 2016

I am a male human being.

And you'd better believe I'm a feminist.

I wear that label proudly.

The other day a friend of mine heard one of my articles was published in Everyday Feminism. And he said, "Kind of a backhanded compliment. Isn't it?"

Hell no!

What does that mean? Would someone suppose that a man being considered a feminist somehow made him less of a man?

On the contrary. I think it makes him more of one. It makes him a decent freakin' person.

I just don't understand this ridicule and fear of being called a feminist. I see it in both men and women.

The other day a co-worker said she's all for the idea that men and women deserve equal pay for the same job, but she doesn't consider herself a feminist.

Why the Hell not? That is a distinctly feminist point of view.

There seems to be this stigma about the term as if being a feminist was tantamount to being some sort of radical troublemaker. Some folks seem to think that feminists essentially hate men and seek them grievous harm.

It's ridiculous.

A feminist is just someone who thinks men and women should have the same rights and opportunities.

That's it. You can add more complicated terms, talk about economic, social and political rights, but it's the same darn thing.

Being a feminist just means you're not an asshole. That's not a gender-specific value. Nor should it depend on your political affiliation, sexual preference or spirituality.

If you think all people, regardless of what they've got between their legs, deserve to be treated fairly, then **SURPRISE!** You're feminist!

In the words of activist and academic Cheris Kramarae, feminism is "the radical notion that women are people."

Some folks try to convince you otherwise. They play a card from the racist playbook. It goes like this:

Stop saying 'Feminism.' Women don't deserve equal rights. All people do.

It's the same passive aggressive trick of the closeted white supremacists who attack Black Lives Matter activists because "All Lives Matter!"

Listen, skeezicks, no one said "**ONLY** Black Lives Matter" just like no one said "**ONLY** women's rights matter." What you're complaining about is pure baloney – a way to shut down the conversation and stop people from talking about inequalities that actually exist for women and people of color.

And don't assume I'm excluding transgender people, either. LGBTs are just as deserving of fair treatment as cisgender folks, heterosexuals or anyone else.

Yes, feminism calls attention to the plight of women. It deserves that attention. We have a lot of work to do making that right. Why should I feel guilty about bringing that up?

I am perfectly comfortable being called a feminist. I have a mother, and I love her. I have two grandmothers, an aunt, a wife, a daughter. Most of us, whether we're women or not, have important relationships with someone of the female persuasion. I can't imagine why anyone would want to deny those loved ones equal treatment.

But you don't have to know or care about a single woman. You could have sprung from the ground like a mushroom and lived in a dark corner without meeting anyone all your life. Why would you want to deny half of the human race fair treatment?

It's a deep seated psychosis. Like so much else, the current Presidential election has brought it even more to the forefront.

For the first time in American history, a woman tops the ticket of a major political party. (She's not even the only one. The Green Party has an impressive female candidate, too!) And just like in 2008 when Barack Obama became the our [sic] first President of color, the crazies are coming out of the woodwork.

I even had a female acquaintance tell me she couldn't support Hillary Clinton because she didn't feel comfortable with a woman in the Oval Office. She thought a woman would be too emotional to make those kinds of life-and-death decisions.

What a pile of crap!

It doesn't matter if you support Clinton or not. Being a woman does not disqualify her from the Presidency. Women make life-and-death decisions every day. In fact, given that many women have the very machinery of life embedded in their own bodies, they may be **MORE** suited to these decisions than men. After all, they are empowered to decide whether new life comes into the world. They literally give birth to the future.

Men can be important parts of the process. But it's not biologically required to the same degree.

Being the father of a daughter is the most important relationship in my life.

And I'll admit it made me think about gender issues more deeply.

All parents see the world anew through their children's eyes, and what I see from my little one's point of view doesn't fill me with confidence.

I see everywhere women have to prove themselves just to get in the door while men are assumed to be worthy of a shot just by virtue of their masculinity.

People listen to men more seriously than they do women. People expect men to take the lead. They expect women to follow. Men have much higher representation in almost all valued professions – doctors, lawyers, politicians.

It's no wonder school teachers get no respect. They're mostly women. As one of the few males in front of the classroom, I see this first hand on a daily basis.

So I try to do what I can to protect my daughter from ingesting these cultural stereotypes and sick ways of thinking.

Just the other day, we were listening to a Joan Jett song, and my little one asked if there were many good women rock stars. I responded by making her a playlist on my iPod filled with nothing but female fronted music groups. It's full of artists like No Doubt, Cyndi Lauper, the Pretenders, Heart, Lauryn Hill, Patti LaBelle and Fiona Apple.

My daughter loves it. When we ride around in the car she invariably asks for "The Girl Album," and I get it. She likes hearing people like her in that role. She likes seeing that it's a possibility, that girls don't have to take a backseat. They can lead. They're just as important as boys any day.

That's what being a feminist means.

It's challenging your own patriarchal ways of thinking. It's continually asking 'Is this fair?" It's having the courage to challenge the status quo and siding with the oppressed against the oppressor – even if the oppressor looks like you.

So Hell Yeah I'm a feminist. And if you're not – really – what is wrong with you!!?

1. Do you think the author's view of feminism is on point, or too simplistic?

2. Earlier commentators have discussed the value of thinking in terms of "advocating feminism" rather than "being a feminist." How does this view bear on the above sentiments?

"ENOUGH OF ANGER: WHY I GAVE UP FEMINIST ACTIVISM," BY FREDERICA MATHEWES-GREEN, FROM THE *NATIONAL REVIEW*, SEPTEMBER 30, 2013

Sorting through some old boxes in the basement, I ran across a manila envelope stuffed with 40-year-old women's-lib literature. It was right under the Earth Shoes. Forty years ago, I was a Mother Earth-type hippie and an enthusiastic "women's libber" (then the term of choice). In the envelope I found an assortment of leaflets protesting the nuclear family (inherently oppressive) and warning against "female hygiene deodorant," "the myth of the vaginal orgasm," and other threats to womankind. There were some huffy letters I'd written to the campus newspaper, and mimeographed flyers for the campus women's group. The pride of the collection was a 1971 copy of the classic feminist guide to health and sexuality, *Our Bodies, Ourselves*. This was the pre-mainstream edition, published by the New England Free Press, stapled together and priced at 40 cents.

Most revealing, though, was an old issue of *Off Our Backs*, the underground newspaper of the radical feminists of Washington, D.C. I was briefly a volunteer on the staff and helped lay out this issue. I saved it because it carried my review of a movie titled "La Salamandre," which I hadn't thought about since.

It was a different world, a moment when hopes were high and the movement was at full boil. We looked ahead to a future very different from the one that came about.

The issue, dated February-March 1973, led with a report on the sixth national conference of NOW, the National Organization for Women. It's a rather cranky report, because the authors were fed up with NOW's being so wishy-washy. You see, at the conference, NOW's president, Wilma Scott Heide, had stated that a "masculine mystique" ruled our society, and that it must be overturned by a "profound universal behavioral revolution." She said that mild forms of social action, such as boycotts, had proven ineffective, so the movement must become more militant—sit-ins, teach-ins, "anything short of violence." For example, the Federal Communications Commission had failed to practice affirmative action, so women should just take over the stations.

Scorn fairly drips from the reporter's pen: "Such tactics are clearly not directed at the liberation of a free space for women, a women's culture, or variants of lesbian separatist proposals, but at joining the 'man's world.'" Indeed, NOW's stated purpose, "to bring women into full participation in the mainstream of American society," is deplorable, in the writer's view: It allows "the basic structure of that society, which necessarily keeps most women in the mainstream of the home and low-paying jobs, to go unchallenged."

This happened to be the first issue after the Roe v. Wade decision, and the writer's opinion was—you guessed it—that Roe didn't go far enough: "What was won was only a significant first start in a continuing struggle." The decision allowed states to regulate abortion in the second and third trimesters, but we must persevere in "making abortions a matter of choice during the entire pregnancy."

Leafing forward, we come to the second installment in a series titled "Experiments in Hostility." The author describes three recent incidents in which she tried to confront sexism: at a party, in a college classroom, and in the studio audience of Dick Cavett's TV show. She recommends hissing. (The article is accompanied by a rather alarming castration cartoon. Hissing is better.)

Much of what we meet on these pages is long gone, and it's a good thing. Lesbian-separatist communities were never going to be more than a gleam in somebody's eye. The odd-looking neologism "chairone" was never likely to replace the old, sexist "chairman"; and "Sappho Was a Right-on Woman" didn't set a new style for edgy book titles. Today, could you call anyone a "male chauvinist pig" with a straight face?

I had completely forgotten about "consciousness-raising groups." These gatherings aimed to be part group therapy and part feminist training, and the NOW convention included a workshop on setting up such groups. But the room was too small, and the audience grew testy and complained they weren't receiving the instruction they needed. One participant pointed out the organizers' error: "The whole point of [consciousness raising] is to change that cast of mind which makes you feel you have to get expert advice for everything. Consciousness raising is not a skill you can learn from experts."

Some of the movement's hopes and plans are almost poignantly absurd. The 18-month goals announced at the NOW conference included "getting rid of sexism on the Dean Martin show, removal of 'My wife, I think I'll keep her' ads by Geritol, and eliminating the blatant sexism in children's TV cartoons and shows."

And did you think Marlo Thomas's album of children's songs, *Free to Be You and Me*, took a progressive, feminist stance? (I sure did; I played it for my children.) Nope, for despite the songs' emphasis on breaking gender stereotypes, most still pair girl characters with boy characters, and thus "assume and reinforce traditional family roles."

Most endearing in this issue was a young woman's notes on her first visits to a lesbian bar. She wore a long skirt the first time, and was immediately asked to dance by a "Bogart-voiced" woman who advised her to try to be "a little butcher." The following week she wore jeans, and "I may as well have had a sex change." The women who had previously asked her to dance ignored her, and the women in skirts expected her to ask them to dance. The entrenched sex-stereotyping does not escape her notice.

The most horrifying entry in this issue (apart from that castration cartoon) is an essay by a woman recounting the misery she endured because it was a holiday and her eight-year-old and her "man" were home for the day. (A female houseguest is also present, but "she has worked on self-development for 10 years now & tends to play less games than most people.") The author dreads the daylong presence of these two people you would assume she loves, but tries to set a positive tone with some piano playing. Soon she is screaming at the man to "get out," but when he complies, she screams that he's a coward and slams his chair around till it's in pieces. At this point, "the kids say o dear & put the chair back together.") She decides to watch TV, but when the eight-year-old tries to quiet the baby, it results in a baby who can't be consoled because she is "too busy suffering full volume." The author turns up the TV volume and stares at the screen "resolutely." When the show is over, she goes out on the patio to scream, "I hate holidays I hate holidays I hate holidays I hate holidays I hate holidays I hate holidays I hate holidays" while the baby cries "momma momma."

The author points out that "everyone has holidays, everyone suffers through them," and must find some way to cope. She concludes that, next holiday, she will take a tranquilizer as soon as she wakes up, and will "refuse to play sacrificial lamb again. Next time I will not be the one to collapse on the patio crying 'how can I fight loneliness when I'm always alone how can I fight loneliness when I'm always alone how can I fight loneliness when I'm always alone how can I fight loneliness when I'm always alone how can I.' Next time if I want to be happy on a goddamn holiday I goddamn will be happy." Whew.

The problem here actually has less to do with feminism specifically than with another social phenomenon of the time: the Human Potential Movement, which sought to unleash the immense potential hidden within each person. The movement's emphasis on getting "real" and revealing your "gut feelings" unfortunately turned some susceptible people into emotional bullies and fountains of self-pity. When it was paired with the "stay angry" element of any liberation movement, it had the potential to unleash some really miserable, and misery-inflicting, personalities.

That was why I began to withdraw from the feminist movement. I did it because I realized I was angry all the time. I was always scrutinizing things for sexism— movies, advertising, conversation, everything. I began to sense how addictive this kind of self-righteous anger can be. It wipes away ambivalence and self-doubt, making guilt feelings unnecessary. I was wronged, the seductive thinking goes, so anything I do is justified. If others think it "wrong," it's only evidence of how much sexism has damaged us all.

I realized that I was turning into a kind of person I didn't want to be and stopped actively participating in feminism, though without changing my opinions. Those were changed later, by the real-life experiences of marriage and child rearing. I was floored to discover that little girls really do prefer dolls and pretty dresses even if you clothe them in blue jeans and keep giving them toy trucks. There was something deeper, more ancient, more body-based in gender roles than I had realized.

That's no excuse for cruelty and injustice, and where there are excesses, it is right to protest and seek change. But I could no longer deny that (most) males and females really like their opposite-ness; they like to joke about and exaggerate it, and this was something feminist theory was never going to be able to change. People savor and celebrate this oppositeness because the difference between the sexes is where new life comes from. Perpetuating the species is serious business, but it's also a source of great joy. This biological reality is so vast and deep in the human race that you just can't fight it. Before long I didn't even want to.

I wonder what happened to all the other women who felt as zealous and uncompromising as I did 40 years ago. As in any population, the majority of us were heterosexual, and that tends to nudge women toward pairing up with a man and having babies. In that process a lot of us found we were longing for things we never expected to want. Whatever our theories, real life had some tricks up its sleeve. I'm glad that it did.

1. The author makes a strong claim for essential difference, rooted in biology, between the sexes. Do you agree?

2. In your opinion, is there anything problematic about dismissing a political movement based on a few crank personalities within it? Does the author's opinion of feminism seem credible and balanced?

CONCLUSION

The feminist movement in America began to truly take shape in the nineteenth and early twentieth centuries. In tandem with the women's suffrage movement, the first wave of feminism secured impressive political gains for women. By the mid nineteenth century, many states allowed women limited rights, such as Maine's provision for "separate economy" (1844), the right to file patents (1848), and the right to hold property. The early feminist movement in the US culminated with the Nineteenth Amendment, which guaranteed all women nationwide the right to vote in 1919.

Even after these important victories, American women still endured subordinate status for much of the twentieth century. During the post-war boom, a second wave of feminism emerged that named and addressed some of the more insidious forms of institutionalized discrimination. These feminists rallied against the stultifying conditions of patriarchy, eventually winning women access to legal abortion in 1971. Furthermore, second-wave feminists were instrumental in demanding equal pay, contraception, child-care, and access to the same opportunities as men. The more radical among them challenged capitalist exploitation, racism, colonialism, and environmental degradation, causes currently championed by feminism's third wave.

Despite much progress, the future of feminism is currently in peril. While intersectional feminism has broadened the theory to diagnose a wide range of societal ills, average women are not completely on board. Many women, perhaps those of unacknowledged privilege, take for granted the difficult struggles their feminist forebears worked so hard to win. Believing that the fight for equality has been settled once and for all, these women see few barriers barring their entry to employment and personal freedom. Of course, this is in many ways both true and a cause for celebration. But one need only take a cursory glance at the many legislative attempts to restrict women's autonomy to realize that progress is not irreversible. Now more than ever, a commitment to the basic beliefs of feminism is crucial to maintain momentum, whether or not one wholeheartedly embraces the feminist label.

For many younger feminists, social media has become an increasingly attractive and effective way to organize and articulate lived experience, and an antidote to articulations of feminism that do not resonate. Many authors we have read have identified the pros and cons of this approach. On the one hand, it allows women to amplify their voices and find the support of like-minded peers. On the other, it encourages a certain enforced conformity, a dangerous tendency toward sensationalism, and a vulnerability to "call-out" culture. Nonetheless, social media fills the void that traditional media has missed by offering more honest depictions of everyday feminism.

It is ironic that a social theory seeking unity can be so divisive. From Facebook groups such as Women Against Feminism to President Donald Trump, feminism faces intense backlash in current America. It has been the aim of this reader to clarify feminism's essential purpose in the hopes of bringing more people on board with this inclusive and overwhelmingly positive movement.

BIBLIOGRAPHY

Ahmad, Aalya. "Feminism Beyond The Waves: Do We Need A Different Metaphor Than Three Big Waves To Appreciate Feminism Today?" *Briarpatch*, June 30, 2015. https://briarpatchmagazine.com/articles/view/feminism-beyond-the-waves.

Azaransky, Sarah. "Jane Crow: Pauli Murray's Intersections and Antidiscrimination Law." *Journal of Feminist Studies in Religion*, vol. 29, no. 1, 2013, pp. 155–160.

Bianco, Marcie. "A Manifesto For All: Bisexual Trans Activist And Author Julia Serano Wants To Make Feminism Inclusive." *Curve*, Volume 26, Issue 5, September–October 2016, p. 28.

Bloom, Peter. "Clinton's Inspiring and Troubling Liberal Feminism." *Common Dreams*, August 02, 2016. http://www.commondreams.org/views/2016/08/02/clintons-inspiring-and-troubling-liberal-feminism.

Brownworth, Victoria A. "Who is Winning the War on Women?: Women's History Month is the Time to Reflect on Our Lack of Progress." *Curve*, Volume 26, Issue 2, March–April 2016, p. 16.

Corvid, Virginia. "Vernacular Third Wave Discourse": New Works On Riot Grrrl, Girl Zines, And Girl Rock. *Feminist Collections: A Quarterly of Women's Studies* Resources, Fall 2010. https://www.library.wisc.edu/gwslibrarian/wp-content/uploads/sites/28/2015/05/FC_314_RiotGrrrl.pdf.

Crane, Connie Jeske. "Social Media As A Feminist Tool." *Herizons*, Fall 2012. http://www.conniejeskecrane.com/uploads/1/4/3/1/14313904/social_media_fall_12.pdf.

Cummins, Denise. "Column: Why Millennial Women Don't Want To Call Themselves Feminists." *PBS News Hour*, February 12, 2016. http://www.pbs.org/newshour/making-sense/column-why-millennial-women-dont-want-to-call-themselves-feminists.

Frankovic, Kathy. "Feminism Today: What Does It Mean?" *Yougov*, August 1, 2014. https://today.yougov.com/news/2014/08/01/feminism-today-what-does-it-mean.

Fulton, Dierdre. "US Supreme Court Stops the Sham by Striking Down Texas Abortion Law." *Common Dreams*, June 27, 2016. http://www.commondreams.org/news/2016/06/27/us-supreme-court-stops-sham-striking-down-texas-abortion-law.

Jabour, Anya. "100 Years of the 'Gender Gap' in American Politics." *The Conversation*, November 24, 2016. https://theconversation.com/100-years-of-the-gender-gap-in-american-politics-67833.

Loreto, Nora. "Feminism's White Default." *Briarpatch*, April 18, 2016. https://briarpatchmagazine.com/articles/view/feminisms-white-default.

Mathewes-Green, Frederica. "Enough Of Anger: Why I Gave Up Feminist Activism." *National Review*, September 30, 2013. https://www.nationalreview.com/nrd/articles/358330/enough-anger.

Myers, Angela. "This is What a Feminist Looks Like: Fighting Racism and Sexism Within the Feminist Movement." *National Organization for Women*, July 13, 2016. http://now.org/blog/this-is-what-a-feminist-looks-like-fighting-racism-and-sexism-within-the-feminist-movement.

Nelson, Rebecca. "The Conservative Answer to Feminism." *National Journal Daily*, May 6, 2015. https://www.nationaljournal.com/s/27427/conservative-answer-feminism.

Rosen, Ruth. "We Never Said "We Wanted it All": How the Media Distorts the Goals of Feminism." *AlterNet*, August 5, 2012. http://www.alternet.org/we-never-said-we-wanted-it-all-how-media-distorts-goals-feminism.

Ruden, Sarah. "Literature, Patriarchy, and Plath." *National Review*, August 10, 2015. https://www.nationalreview.com/nrd/articles/421572/literature-patriarchy-and-plath.

Schaeffer-Duffy, Claire. "Feminists Weigh In On Draft Registration For Women." *National Catholic Reporter*, June 28, 2016. https://www.ncronline.org/news/politics/feminists-weigh-draft-registration-women.

Silman, Anna. "The Election Inspired These 9 Women to Fight Back Against Misogyny in Their Own Lives." *New York Magazine*, October 18, 2016. http://nymag.com/thecut/2016/10/how-trump-inspired-9-women-to-fight-back-against-misogyny.html.

Singer, Steven. "If You're Not a Feminist – What the Hell is Wrong with You!!?" *Common Dreams,* September 10, 2016. http://www.commondreams.org/views/2016/09/10/if-youre-not-feminist-what-hell-wrong-you.

Spar, Debora L. "Shedding the Superwoman Myth." *The Chronicle of Higher Education*, September 2, 2013. http://www.chronicle.com/article/Where-Feminism-Went-Wrong/141293.

Swers, Michele L. "What Trump's Election Could Mean for Women: Fewer Reproductive Rights, New Help for Working Families?" *The Conversation*, November 15, 2016. https://theconversation.com/what-trumps-election-could-mean-for-women-fewer-reproductive-rights-new-help-for-working-families-67531.

Taylor, Scott. "Calling All Men — Five Ways You Can Be a Feminist at Work." *The Conversation*, August 2, 2016. https://theconversation.com/calling-all-men-five-ways-you-can-be-a-feminist-at-work-61403.

Taylor, Stephanie. "#Feminism: Critics Of Social Media Say It's Nothing But White Noise — But It Can Also Amplify Women's Voices." *This Magazine,* March 16, 2015. https://this.org/2015/03/16/feminism.

Teekah, Alyssa. "Lessons From SlutWalk: How Call-Out Culture Hurts Our Movement." *Herizons*, Vol. 29, No. 2, Fall 2015, p. 16.

"Why We Need the Equal Rights Amendment." *Alice Paul Institute (API).* http://www.equalrightsamendment.org/why.htm.

CHAPTER NOTES

CHAPTER 3: WHAT THE COURTS SAY

"JANE CROW: PAULI MURRAY'S INTERSECTIONS AND ANTIDISCRIMINATION LAW" BY SARAH AZARANSKY

(1) Pauli Murray, *Song in a Weary Throat: An American Pilgrimage* (San Francisco: Harper & Row, 1987), 271.
(2) Pauli Murray, "Why Negro Girls Stay Single," *Negro Digest* 5, no. 9 (1947): 5.
(3) Pauli Murray, "The Right to Equal Opportunity in Employment," *California Law Review* 33 (1945): 388-433, and Pauli Murray, *States' Laws on Race and Color* (Cincinnati: Women's Division of Christian Service, Board of Missions and Church Extension, Methodist Church, 1951), and Pauli Murray and Leslie Rubin, *The Constitution and Government of Ghana* (London: Sweet and Maxwell, 1964).
(4) Serena Mayeri, *Reasoning from Race: Feminism, Law, and the Civil Rights Revolution* (Cambridge, MA: Harvard University Press, 2011), 2.
(5) Ibid., 14.
(6) Pauli Murray, "Memorandum in Support of Retaining the Amendment to H.R. 7152, Title VII (Equal Employment Opportunity) To Prohibit Discrimination in Employment Because of Sex," April 14, 1964, 9, Pauli Murray Papers, Schlesinger Library, Radcliffe Institute, Harvard University, Cambridge, MA.
(7) Ibid., 21.
(8) Ibid., 20.
(9) Kimberle Crenshaw, "Demarginalizing the Intersection of Race and Sex: A Black Feminist Critique of Antidiscrimination Doctrine, Feminist Theory, and Antiracist Politics," *University of Chicago Legal Forum* (1989): 140.
(10) *DeGraffenreid v. General Motors*, US Court of Appeals, 8th Circuit, July 15, 1977.
(11) Minna Kotkin, "Diversity and Discrimination: A Look at Complex Bias," *William and Mary Law Review* 50, no. 5 (2009): 1439-1500, quotation on 1443.
(12) Ibid., 1439.

(13) Rachel Best et al., "Multiple Disadvantage: An Empirical Test of Intersectionality Theory in EEO Litigation," *Law and Society Review* 45, no. 4 (December 2011): 991-1025, quotation on 992.
(14) I am indebted to Traci West for the term *common freedom struggle*, which she defines as a "struggle that women jointly share-one that directly attends to the racist realities in the politics of their histories," in Traci C. West, "Extending Black Feminist Sisterhood in the Face of Violence: Fanon, White Women, and Veiled Muslim Women," in *Convergences: Black Feminism and Continental Philosophy*, ed. Maria del Guadalupe Davidson, Kathryn T. Gines, and Donna-Dale L. Marcano, SUNY Series in Gender Theory (Albany: SUNY Press, 2010), 176.
(15) Genna Rae McNeill, "Interview with Pauli Murray," February 13, 1976, p. 89, Southern Oral History Program University of North Carolina at Chapel Hill.
(16) Ibid.
(17) Cornel West, *Keeping Faith: Philosophy and Race in America* (New York: Routledge, 1993), 240, 247, 271.

CHAPTER 5: WHAT THE MEDIA SAY

"'VERNACULAR THIRD WAVE DISCOURSE': NEW WORKS ON RIOT GRRRL, GIRL ZINES, AND GIRL ROCK" BY VIRGINIA CORVID

(1.) Band and zine references refer predominantly to projects contemporaneous with the heyday of Riot Grrrl. All artists referenced in this review have been involved with multiple projects, too many to list. Googling them yields rich returns and is highly recommended by this reviewer.
(2.) Riot Grrrl sought to avoid hegemonic doctrine and encouraged all participants to develop their own notion of Riot Grrrl. Many Riot Grrrl participants therefore developed "Riot Grrrl is ..." manifestos, so many, indeed, that the term manifesta has since found widespread usage. By far the most widely published Riot Grrrl manifesta, however, appeared in the zine *Bikini Kill*

2, the compelling prose and vision of which has engendered its continued prominence. The full text is available at **http://onewar-art.org/riot_grrrl_manifesto.htm.manifesto.htm**. Note: this site erroneously claims that Kathleen Hanna founded Riot Grrrl, a claim that runs counter to the spirit of Riot Grrrl and that Hanna herself has spent a considerable amount of time contesting.

GLOSSARY

ableism—Discrimination or prejudice against individuals with disabilities.

activism—A policy of action to achieve a political or social goal.

activist—A reformer and agent of change for social causes.

Betty Friedan—American feminist who founded a national organization for women and wrote *The Feminine Mystique* (1963), which is generally credited as a major impetus for second-wave of feminist political struggle.

biphobia—Aversion toward bisexuality and bisexual people as a social group or as individuals.

bisexuality—An identity for which sex and gender are not a boundary to attraction.

cisgender—Denoting or relating to a person whose self-identity conforms with the gender that corresponds to their sex.

double standard—A set of principles that applies differently and usually more rigorously to one group of people or circumstances than to another; especially a code of morals that applies more severe standards of sexual behavior to women than to men.

heteronormative—Of, relating to, or based on the attitude that heterosexuality is the only normal and natural expression of sexuality.

heterosexual—To be sexually attracted to people of the opposite sex; based on sexual attraction to people of the opposite sex.

homophobia—Irrational fear of, aversion to, or discrimination against homosexuality and gay men or women.

gay—The term for same-sex attraction, sexual orientation, and identity for men and women who are attracted to the same sex.

intersectionality—A concept often used in critical theories to describe the ways in which oppressive institutions (racism, sexism, homophobia, transphobia, ableism, xenophobia, classism, etc.) are interconnected and cannot be examined separately from one another.

misogyny—A hatred of women.

patriarchy—A social organization marked by the leading role of the father in the family and the legal dependence of wives and children; simply stated, the inordinate power held by men over women in certain societies.

privilege—A set of advantages (or lack of disadvantages) enjoyed by a majority group.

racism—A belief that certain races are superior to other races.

rape culture—A society in which rape is pervasive and normalized due to societal attitudes about gender, sex, and sexuality.

sexism—Prejudice or discrimination based on sex; especially discrimination against women; behavior, conditions, or attitudes that foster stereotypes of social roles based on sex.

slut-shaming—Attacking a woman or a girl for being sexual, having one or more sexual partners, acknowledging sexual feelings, and/or acting on sexual feelings.

transgender—A person who identifies with or expresses a gender identity that differs from the one which corresponds to the person's [assigned] sex at birth.

transphobia—The intense dislike of or prejudice against transgender people.

victim-blaming—When the victim of a crime or accident is held as wholly or partially responsible for the wrongful conduct committed against them.

wage gap—The difference between the amounts of money paid to women and men, often for doing the same work.

white feminism—A set of beliefs that allows for the exclusion of issues that specifically affect women of color; a feminism in which middle class white women are the mold that others must fit.

FOR MORE INFORMATION

Butler, Judith. *Gender Trouble*. New York, NY: Routledge, 2009.

Davis, Angela. *Women, Race, and Class*. New York, NY: Vintage Books, 1981.

de Beauvoir, Simone. *The Second Sex*. New York, NY: Penguin Books, 1954.

Gilbert, Sandra. *Feminist Literary Theory and Criticism*. New York, NY: Norton, 2007.

Halberstam, Jack. *Gaga Feminism*. New York, NY: Beacon Press, 2013.

Hesford, Victoria. *Feeling Women's Liberation*. Chapel Hill, NC: Duke UP, 2013.

hooks, bell. *Ain't I a Woman: Black Women and Feminism*. Chicago, IL: South End Press, 1999.

Mulvey, Laura. *Visual and Other Pleasures*. London: Palgrave, 2009.

Needson, Premilla. *Household Workers Unite: The Untold Story of African American Women Who Built a Movement*. New York, NY: Beacon Press, 2015.

Showalter, Elaine. *A Literature of Their Own*. Princeton, NJ: Princeton UP, 1985.

Smith, Andrea. *Conquest: Sexual Violence and American Indian Genocide*. Chapel Hill, NC: Duke UP, 2015.

Woolf, Virginia. *A Room of One's Own*. London: Albatross Publishers, 2015.

WEBSITES

Alice Paul Institute (ERA)
www.alicepaul.org

The Alice Paul Institute is a non-profit dedicated to feminist
suffragette Alice Paul's vision of gender equality, particularly
in the American political process. It is based in Mount Laurel,
New Jersey, at Alice Paul's birthplace.

The Equal Rights Amendment (ERA)
www.equalrightsamendment.org

This is the official website for the Equal Rights Amendment
(ERA), the proposed Amendment to the Constitution that
would guarantee that all rights could not be denied based on
one's sex or gender. The ERA has been introduced into every
Congress since its initial passage by Congress in 1972. For
official inclusion into the Constitution, it would need to be
ratified by thirty-eight of fifty states.

The Feminist Majority Foundation (FMF)
www.feminist.org

The Feminist Majority Foundation is a consciousness-raising
group that draws inspiration from the fact that 56 percent of
American women self-identify as feminists. Founded in 1987,
it is dedicated to promoting women's equality, reproductive
health, and non-violence through research, education,
and action.

INDEX